William Thompson

The History and Antiquities of the Collegiate Church of St. Saviour

(St. Marie Overie), Southwark

William Thompson

The History and Antiquities of the Collegiate Church of St. Saviour
(St. Marie Overie), Southwark

ISBN/EAN: 9783337002466

Printed in Europe, USA, Canada, Australia, Japan

Cover: Foto ©ninafisch / pixelio.de

More available books at **www.hansebooks.com**

THE
HISTORY AND ANTIQUITIES
OF THE
COLLEGIATE
Church of St. Saviour
(St. Marie Overie),
SOUTHWARK

(With Thirty two Illustrations.)

BY THE

REV. CANON THOMPSON, M.A., D.D.,

Rector of St. Saviour's, and Chancellor of the Collegiate Church.

LONDON:
Printed and Published by ASH & CO., Ltd., 42, Southwark Street. S.E

1898.

PREFACE.

THE larger Edition, and the Edition with Appendix, of "The History and Antiquities of the Collegiate Church of St. Saviour (St. Marie Overie), Southwark," being now out of print, the present revised Epitome is issued in order to save the visitor from being misled by inefficient and inaccurate "Guides to London."

The letterpress portion brings the history up to the present time, and although one or two of the illustrations belong to the period anterior to the restoration of the Church, it has been thought advisable, nevertheless, to retain them, in order that the structural and other alterations which have been effected may be the more clearly seen and noted.

For illustrations of an excellent character, and up to date, the reader is referred to Mr. Dovaston's small *Book of Views* of St. Saviour's, with "Notes" by the present writer. The one book may be regarded as the complement of the other, and both may be obtained in the Vestry of the Parish Church.

N.B.—A fresh issue of the large edition, referred to above, thoroughly revised, and containing much additional matter, and many new illustrations, is in course of preparation, and will appear shortly, when some further contemplated alterations in the Church shall have been carried out.

Dedicated
to
Evelyn Irene:
Amy Beatrice:
and
Ida Marie Overie.

ARMS OF  THE PRIORY.

Argent, a cross fusilly, in the dexter chief a cinquefoil gules.

Past and Present.

A SUMMARY.

THIS CHURCH is considered to be the finest mediæval building in London after Westminster Abbey. It has a record of more than a thousand years, interwoven with much that is interesting in history, literature, and legend. Stow* relates, on the authority of Linstede, the last prior, that, "East from the Bishop of *Winchester's* house, directly over against it, standeth a fair Church called S. Mary Over the *Rie*, or Overy, that is, over the water.† This Church, or some

---

* John Stow, b. 1525. d. 1605: *Survey of London*, p. 449 (Ed. 1633).

† The more correct derivation is as follows. *Ōfer*, in Old English, signifies a river-bank or shore ; and *ie*, an island or land by water. So that St. Mary Overie would mean the Church dedicated to the Blessed Virgin Mary, situated on "the water-land by the river-bank," that is, *St. Mary of Bankside*, the old Roman Embankment.

Previous to the 15th century it appears to have been known invariably as "St. Mary, Suthwerche." In the Appendix (Part I.) to the *Ninth Report Hist. MSS. Comm*, 5 b, it is so named in 1162 ; also in 1260. In a document dated at the Lateran, in 1300, it is " St. Mary, Southwark," (*ib.* 6a). Brother Robert de Welles (1331-1348) is mentioned as Prior of the Convent

other in place thereof, was (of old time, long before the Conquest) a house of Sisters, founded by a Maiden, named *Mary*, unto the which house of Sisters she left (as was left to her by her Parents) the oversight and profits of a Cross Ferry, or traverse, over the *Thames*, there kept before that any Bridge was builded." This House of Sisters was afterwards converted by St. Swithun, who was Bishop of Winchester from 852 to 862, into a College of Priests. Hence the Church is still styled "Collegiate." And from that time onwards the Church has owed almost everything to successive Bishops of Winchester. Bishop Giffard, assisted by two Norman Knights, William of Pont de l'Arche and William Dauncey, built the original Norman Nave in 1106, and Canons Regular of the Order of St. Augustine* were established, the Collegiate Church becoming a monastery. Bishop Peter de Rupibus (*alias* de la Roche) built the Choir and Ladye Chapel in 1207, and altered the Norman character of the Nave, which had suffered from fire, into Early English. The nave once more suffered from fire in the time of Richard II., and in his reign and in that of Henry IV., perpendicular work was introduced into it. Gower, the poet, and Cardinal Beaufort were liberal benefactors to the Church at this period, the former founding the Chantry of St. John, and the latter restoring the South Transept at his own cost. The roof of the Nave, which was of stone, fell in 1469, and an oak roof, groined, was substituted, some of the quaint bosses of which may be still seen. The magnificent Altar Screen is due to Bishop Fox (1520). The old Nave

---

of "St. Mary, Southwark" (*ib.* 16a), Werkeworth (1414-1452) is also described as Prior of "St. Mary, Southwark" (*ib.* 16 b).

In a 15th century MS., however, it is styled "St. Mary Overeye, in Southwark," (*ib.* 17a). This last name clung to it long after the Reformation. See Pepys' *Diary*, July 3, 1663. See also, *infra*, p. 69 (note †).

I may be allowed to refer, for further particulars, as to the meaning of *Overie*, to my contribution to *Notes and Queries*, 1895, p. 340.

* They were styled *Black Canons* from the colour of their habit. As an Order they occupied a middle position between monks and the secular (parochial) clergy, and almost resembled a community of parish priests living under rule. Postulants for admission to the order professed the usual vows of Poverty, Chastity, and Obedience, in the following terms: Ego Frater N. offero me serviturum sub canonica regula beati Augustini *sine proprietate, in castitate*, et promitto *obedienciam* domino N. priori. (J. Willis Clark: *Customs of Augustinian Canons*, p. 134).

again fell into decay, and was allowed to remain a roofless ruin for many years, until in 1838 it was taken down, when many remains of ancient Norman work were shamelessly broken up and scattered. The foundation stone of a debased and flimsy Nave was laid by Dr. Sumner, Bishop of Winchester, in 1839, A memorial stone of greater promise was laid on the same site July 24th, 1890, by H.R.H. the Prince of Wales, accompanied by T.R.H. the Princess of Wales and the young Princesses Victoria and Maud.

The Church is cruciform, and, including the walls and buttresses is nearly 300 feet long and about 130 feet broad, and consists of Ladye Chapel and Choir (Early English), Transepts (Decorated), Nave (Early English), and a noble Tower (the upper stages Perpendicular, the lowest Decorated) 35 feet square, and, with pinnacles, 163 feet high, and contains a fine peal of twelve bells, the total weight being over 215 cwt., the tenor being over 51 cwt. In 1424, in the time of Prior Werkeworth, the original peal consisted of seven, which were recast of greater weight in the same year. Each bell had a name, such as Augustine, Maria, &c.

In 1540 the Priory Church and Rectory were *leased* from the Crown to the parishioners at an annual rental of about fifty pounds, and St. Marie Overie became St. Saviour, Bishop Gardiner lending a helping hand. This lease was renewed from time to time, until in 1614 the Church was *purchased* by them from the King in the name of nineteen " bargainers," or trustees, for eight hundred pounds. The parishioners continued to be patrons of the living until 1885, when, by an Act of Parliament, the right of presentation was vested in the Bishop of the Diocese, and the Chaplain made Rector.

Intimately connected with this Church and parish were Chaucer, Alexander Cruden, Dr. Samuel Johnson, Oliver Goldsmith, Baxter and Bunyan, whom, it will be seen, it is proposed to honour with memorial windows in the north aisle of the Nave.

Three Lord Mayors of London are interred here (Bromfield, 1658; Waterman, 1682; Shorter, 1688) without memorials of any kind: and three Bishops (Sandall, 1319; Wickham ii., 1595; and Andrewes, 1626), the first two also without monument or inscription.

It was here that Boniface, Archbishop of Canterbury,

consecrated Henry de Wengham to London in 1260, and another to St. Asaph in 1268. It was here that Edingdon, Bishop of Winchester, consecrated John de St. Paul to Dublin in 1350, and John de Sheppey to Rochester in 1353, two others in 1355, and another in 1362. It was here that Gardiner consecrated six Bishops on the same day in 1554. And it was in the Chapel of the Bishop of Winchester's London Palace, which for centuries stood close to the west end of this Church, two others were consecrated, one in 1634, and the other in 1635. (See Bishop Stubb's *Registrum Sacrum Anglicanum*, *passim*.) And it was in the same chapel that the great William of Wykeham was ordained Acolyte, Subdeacon and Priest (p. 41).

It should be mentioned that Gower, the father of English poetry, and Massinger, and Fletcher, and Edmond Shakespeare (brother of the great dramatist) are buried here. It was here, in 1406, the Earl of Kent, grandson of the "Fair Maid of Kent," was united in wedlock to Lucia, eldest daughter of the Lord of Milan, Henry IV. giving the bride away at the Church door;* it was here, in 1423 (Henry VI.) that James I. of Scotland, the Royal poet, was married to Joan, niece of Cardinal Beaufort; it was here that Bishop Gardiner condemned the Anglican Martyrs to death in 1555; it was here that Queen Elizabeth assisted at the Earl of Cumberland's wedding; it was here, in Montague Close, the site of the old Cloisters, tradition has it, that Monteagle received his warning letter about the Gunpowder Plot; it was here that John Harvard, the founder of the great American University which bears his name, was baptised, November 29th, 1607; and it was here that the famous Dr. Henry Sacheverell was elected Chaplain in 1705.

---

*Anciently the Marriage Ceremony commenced at the Porch *(ante ostium ecclesiæ)*, or in some portion of the Nave, and was concluded at the Altar; a custom which still prevails in some Yorkshire, Lincolnshire, and Somersetshire Churches, and elsewhere. Chaucer, in his *Canterbury Tales*, makes the wife of Bath say—

"Housebondes atté *Chirch dore* I have had fyve."

Tour of the Interior.

ON entering by the South Transept door, there will be noticed, affixed to a pillar immediately on the right, the armorial bearings, surmounted by a Cardinal's hat, of the distinguished ecclesiastic and statesman,

Cardinal Beaufort.

ROYAL ARMS
OF

HENRY
BEAUFORT

3

HIS father, John of Gaunt, Duke of Lancaster, was married three times. By his first wife he had an only son, who became Henry IV., and by his third he had Henry Beaufort, who was, therefore, half brother to the king. He derived his name from Beaufort Castle, in France, the place of his birth. He became Lord Chancellor, Bishop of Winchester in 1404, Cardinal in 1427, died in 1447, and lies buried in Winchester Cathedral. He was known as the "rich Cardinal," and is credited with having rebuilt this South Transept at his own cost, after the ruins of a great fire.

In order to strengthen his house by a powerful alliance,

and, perhaps, also with a view of uniting the crowns of England and Scotland, he was instrumental in effecting the marriage of his niece, Joan, daughter of his own brother, Sir John Beaufort, Earl of Somerset, to James I. of Scotland. It is a story of romance and tragedy. The young Prince, in his flight, at the age of 13, to the Court and Schools of France, was driven by a storm on the English coast, captured and detained a prisoner (with much liberty and kindness, however) in Windsor Castle for about 18 years. "Stone walls do not a prison make," but shortly before his release he found himself a willing captive to the charms of the fair Princess—

"Such a lord is Love;
And Beauty such a mistress of the world."

He was a poet, and sang of her beauty to the music of his harp, an instrument in the playing of which he is said to have possessed unrivalled skill. His cruel murder in the Dominican Monastery at Perth terminated a happy union, after which Joan married Sir James Stewart, the Black Knight of Lorn.

Emerson.

OPPOSITE the Cardinal's coat of arms, on the west wall of this Transept, is a monument to William Emerson, consisting of an emaciated, diminutive, recumbent effigy (a *memento mori*), with an inscription which tells us that he reached the ripe old age of 92, and that—

"He lived and died an honest man."

His grandson, Thomas Emerson, was a liberal benefactor to the poor of our parish, and his munificence, bestowed in 1620, is still enjoyed by several pensioners of his bounty. He, too, "lived and died an honest man,' and charitable withal.

"A prince can make a belted knight,
A marquis, duke, and a' that;
But an honest man's aboon his might—
Guid faith, he maunna fa' that."

Ralph Waldo Emerson, b. Boston, U.S.A., 1803, graduate of Harvard University, and essayist, is supposed to have sprung from this good Southwark stock.

Benefield.

TO the right of Emerson, above, is a stilted and curious epitaph in Latin: "These be the incinerated remains of Richard Benefield, Associate of Gray's Inn. To them, after they were thoroughly purified by the frankincense of his piety, the nard of his probity, the amber of his faithfulness, and the oil of his charity, his relatives, friends, the poor, everyone in fact, have added the sweet-scented myrrh of their commendation, and the fresh balsam of their tears." He belonged to a family of Shakespearean actors.

To the left is

Bingham.

HE was saddler to Queen Elizabeth and James I.: one of the "bargainers" or trustees to whom the Church was conveyed by the latter monarch for a sum of money, large in those days, subscribed by the parishioners. He was a good friend to this Parish, and to St. Saviour's Grammar School.

Tree of Jesse.

THE great window in the south, by Kempe, is the gift of Sir Frederick Wigan, Bart., in memory of his daughter. Its tracery, although new, is modelled after the original design, and the subject is the "Tree of Jesse." The "Jesse Tree" is an ancient mode (dating from the thirteenth century) of setting forth the regal genealogy of Jesus, in illustration of the words " There shall come forth a rod out of the stem of Jesse." At the base of the central light Jesse sleeps, his head resting on his hand, and out of his side there springs a vine which spreads out all over the window in branch, and leaf, and fruit. Above Jesse is his son, King David, and above David, the Virgin and Child, suggesting the double dedication of the Church, St. Mary, the original title, and St. Saviour, the name bestowed upon it at the Reformation. The other figures represent the chief Kingly ancestors of Christ, as given in the first chapter of St. Matthew.

This is one of the finest specimens of glass-painting in the Kingdom.

The eastern door in this transept is quite a new introduction; and the organ chamber, with one large opening towards the west and two smaller ones into the choir, is a fresh structure, although it stands on a portion of the site of the St. Mary Magdalene Chapel, which dated from the thirteenth century, but was removed in 1822.

The New Organ (by Lewis) is the noble gift bestowed upon the Church by Mrs. Robert Courage, "regardless of expense," in memory of her husband. It contains more than 4,000 pipes, and with extras, has cost nearly £6,000. Great difficulty was experienced in finding a suitable site for it. A strong attempt was made to place it in the great tower arch leading to the north transept. A few, however, felt that in that position it would mar the rare beauty of that part of the Church. The organ in Chester Cathedral occupies a similar position, but Dr. Bridge, whose opinion was invited, wrote to say that " from a musical point of view such an arrangement was most unsatisfactory." Finally it was resolved to build a chamber for it, the donor generously offering to bear the additional expense that would be incurred. The action is electrical, and the wind is supplied by hydraulic pressure.

"As I passed through this venerable edifice I noticed that the great window of the South Transept was of plain glass, as if Providence had designed that some day the Sons of Harvard should place there a worthy memorial of one who is so well entitled to their veneration." Hy. F. Waters, M.A. (a distinguished American antiquary), in *The New England Historical and Genealogical Register*, July, 1885, p. 281.

The Sons of Harvard have lost *this* opportunity.

4. SOUTH TRANSEPT. Before the Restoration. Note the stone coffin on the floor, beneath this window.

IN this transept will also be observed a fine window, by Kempe, in memory of

Elizabeth Newcomen,

who was laid to rest here, November 20, 1675, but the exact spot is unknown. She was a generous educational and charitable benefactress of the parish. The cost of the memorial has been defrayed by the Governors; old and present scholars of the foundation which still bears her name; and by the parishioners. In allusion to the name of our benefactress, St. Elizabeth occupies the base of the central light as the leading figure, supported on the one hand by that wise King who foreshadowed the "Greater than Solomon," and on the other by Zechariah, who spake of Christ as "The Branch." And so, by this title of the Messiah, and in other ways, this window is linked on to its magnificent neighbour, the "Tree of Jesse." Above St. Elizabeth is her son, St. John the Baptist, supported by Elijah, his prototype, and Malachi, who prophesied of the Forerunner of the Saviour. It is intended that all the windows in this transept shall be devoted to illustrating the Incarnation of our Lord.

It was unveiled by H.R.H. the Duke of Connaught, June 22nd, 1898.

Tesseræ.

MOVING towards the South Aisle of the Nave, and looking east, we have an excellent view of the South Aisle of the Choir, and beyond into the Ladye Chapel, terminating with its window of three sharply-defined lancet lights—the architectural Three in One. As we enter this Aisle we may recognise at our feet a token of the great antiquity of the site of this Church and its surroundings—some Roman tesseræ found about fifty years ago in digging a grave in the south-east angle of the churchyard, where more of the same kind remain. It was the custom of the Roman army, in their marches, to carry such materials in order to pave the spot where the prætorium or general's tent was erected. Many other remains of Roman antiquity have been discovered from time to time in the parish, such as coins, cinerary urns, lachrymatories, terra-cotta sepulchral urns, etc. In examining the foundations of

5 SOUTH AISLE OF CHOIR.

the new Nave, and making excavations here and there, a few pieces of Roman pottery were brought to light. *Stoney Street*, which runs through the adjacent market, also commemorates the Roman occupation. The Romans, it is well known, taught the Ancient Britons to develop the resources of this country. They opened up the island by making roads paved with *stone*. These roads were called *strata*, hence our word *street*.

The Non-Such of the World.

Immediately on the left is a brass—the only one of any antiquity in the Church—with the following quaint inscription:—

SVSANNAH BARFORD,

DEPARTED THIS LIFE THE 20TH OF AVGVST 1652.

AGED 10 YEARS 13 WEEKES,

THE NON-SVCH OF THE WORLD FOR PIETY AND VIRTVE.

IN SOE TENDER YEARS.

AND DEATH AND ENVYE BOTH MVST SAY 'TWAS FITT,
HER MEMORY SHOULD THUS IN BRASSE BEE WRITT.

HERE LIES INTER'D WITHIN THIS BED OF DVST
A VIRGIN PVRE NOT STAIN'D WITH CARNALL LVST
SVCH GRACE THE KING OF KINGS BESTOW'D VPON HER
THAT NOW SHE LIVES WITH HIM A MAID OF HONOVR
HER STAGE WAS SHORT, HER THREAD WAS QVICKLY SPVN,
DRAWNE OVT, AND CVT. GOTT HEAV'N, HER WORK WAS DONE
THIS WORLD TO HER WAS BVT A TRAGED PLAY,
SHE CAME AND SAW'T, DISLIK'T, AND PASS'D AWAY.

Abraham Newland.

BEYOND the door of this Aisle, and between the lancet and the next window, there is a plain slab fixed in obscurity on the wall, to the memory of this remarkable man. He was born in this parish (1730), and his baptism and burial (1807), are recorded in our registers. According to a memoir of him in the writer's possession, published the year after his death, his father belonged to Bucks, was twice married, and had twenty-five children.

Abraham entered the Bank of England as clerk, and rose to the position of Chief Cashier. For 25 years he never once slept out of the building. He died two months after retiring from his post, bequeathing £60,000 in the Stocks to his landlady, whose gratitude is represented by the mean tablet before us. Although he had many friends, he was not so vain as to imagine they would dissolve in tears at the news of his death, and he wrote this epitaph (which, I need hardly say, is not on the monument), for himself shortly before his death:—

"Beneath this stone old Abraham lies:
Nobody laughs, and nobody cries,
Where he is gone, and how he fares,
No one knows, and no one cares."

Moved by the memory of so faithful a servant, perhaps the Governors of the Bank of England will one day come over and help us.

A bank-note was styled an "Abraham Newland," none being genuine without his signature. This explains the saying of Upton:

"I have heard people say *Sham Abram* you may,
But must not sham Abraham Newland."

To *Sham Abram* signified to feign illness in order to avoid work.

George Gwilt.

THE next window is altogether eccentric and kaleidoscopic, and hurts the eye, as a discordant note the ear, and is altogether out of harmony with the sound reputation of the Southwark Architect who loved the place and this House so well, and who, during the restoration of the Ladye Chapel (1832), gave his services gratuitously. He lies entombed in the churchyard outside this window, and there is a tablet of polished granite, heart-shaped, behind the screen which records his self-denying work.

ALTAR SCREEN.
Tomb of Humble. Triforium. Clerestory.

Turning the back on Gwilt's window, we have a striking view of the Screen, with Altar-Tomb, part of Triforium, and Clerestory.

From here we pass into

The Ladye Chapel.

THIS portion of our Church has a three-fold claim upon our attention.

First, because of its unique architectural beauty. All the chief writers on St. Saviour's, whether architects, artists, or

7   LADYE CHAPEL (SOUTH-WEST).
Tomb of Bishop Andrewes. Blank Windows, once open, with Decorated Tracery *temp.* Ed. III. Carved Oak Bosses (removed to another part).

antiquaries, experience much difficulty in giving adequate expression to their admiration of it. They declare that whatever excellencies may have been noticed in the other parts of the building, it would appear that an attempt has been here made to concentrate them in the elegant simplicity of its harmonized design, and the admirable principles of its scientific construction, its slender pillars with their shafts, detached* at the four cardinal points, and the beautiful groinings of the vaulted roof, its single and triple lancet windows of the most perfect symmetry, the correctness of its proportions, and the accuracy of its details combine to render it such a pure, chaste specimen of the Early English style as to make it difficult to find its equal anywhere.

One distinguished antiquary speaks of it as "One of the most chaste and elegant examples of the early pointed architecture of the 13th century in the country; for soon after the simplicity of design became florid and overlaid." Another *(Gent. Mag.* 1832*)* says: "In the solid pillars and acute arches, in the lancet windows, and simple groined roof, may be viewed an unaltered building of the 13th century. The groins of the Chapel are perfect, and extremely beautiful. Corresponding to the four gables without, are four aisles within, the outer ones continuous with the north and south aisles of the choir and nave, and from east to west three aisles." Nor will Mr. Dollman come behind any in his admiration, for he writes: "They who designed this beautiful retro-choir† were artists in the truest sense of the word, for viewed from whatever point, its picturesque charm, gracefulness of design, and merits of detail, alike bear witness to the superior intelligence of the minds that conceived and the hands that executed it."

This Chapel affords an interesting illustration, which may be taken in at a glance, of the progress of the pointed style. We have first the simple lancet-like window with the tooth

---

* In early English work the shafts are often detached, but in Decorated attached.

† Southwark folk, and many others, will find it extremely difficult to abandon the charming name by which it is generally known, and which it has borne from time immemorial, in favour of the cold technical designation above.—*Vide* p. 29.

ornament,* standing alone, and the triple lancet, grouped and bound together by an enclosing arch (Early English): then the two three-light windows with mullions† and tracery (Transitional),‡ that on the south geometrical, with its circles, quatrefoils, etc., that on the north reticulated, slightly more elaborate, and later: after this, the blank windows at the back of the Screen, with their more graceful lines, sometimes called "flowing tracery," and by the French "flamboyant" (flame-like), belonging to the Decorated Period of Edward III.

It is remarkable, in the second place, as having been the scene of the trial and condemnation of the

Anglican Martyrs

in 1555, a memorable date in the history of our Church, and in the annals of our country. Beneath that three-light window in the north-east bay of this Chapel, sat in that year, Stephen Gardiner, Bishop of Winchester, and his fellow commissioners, Dr. Bonner, Bishop of London, and others, acting under authority from the See of Rome, and of Mary and her obsequious Parliament, to try certain Prelates, Dignitaries and Priests of the Church of England, whose only crime, apparently, consisted in a stout resistance to the usurpations of the Papal Schism. It was here they witnessed a brave confession, and from here they went forth to receive their baptism of fire. We are bound to honour these men, notwithstanding the occasional extravagancy of language and opinion to which they gave vent under examination, remembering the terrible crisis they had to face, which was nothing less than the deliberate and powerful attempt to re-impose the Vatican yoke upon our Apostolic Church.

---

* Resembling a row of teeth, sometimes called Dog's Tooth, and Shark's Tooth, and the Diagonal Flower. By French antiquaries it is named *Violette*, as it often bears considerable likeness to that flower when half expanded.

† *Mullion*, the vertical bar dividing the light of a window.

‡ The work executed when one style was merging into the next is known as Transitional.

| They are sometimes, but erroneously, styled "Protestant" Martyrs. This was a struggle maintained by Churchmen from beginning to end. Protestantism, in the sense of Separatism, had no existence in this country before the time of Elizabeth.

8   Scene of the Trial.

Ladye Chapel (North-East). Piscina. Stone Coffin (removed). Underneath is an Easter Sepulchre.

It is well, however, to remember that the religious tenets which these men professed were importations from Holland and Switzerland, and other parts of the Continent. Their doctrine was not of native growth; and, had it prevailed, the Church of England would have lost its Catholicity, and been nothing more than a Church "made in Germany."

Seven of the numerous band of Martyrs of Mary's reign are commemorated here in six lancet lights, three on the north-east, and three on the south-east; and by that atrocious blur and blot and daub on the south—a crime and sin against every canon of good taste and feeling.

It would be doing the Marian Martyrs, who are here represented, a vast honour to remove their present crude, inartistic windows, and replace them with others of real merit. The new windows would of course be in memory of the same seven men.

Space will not permit us to add much more than their names:—

1. Rev. Lawrence Saunders, Rector of Allhallows. Bread Street. Burned at Coventry.
2. The Right Rev. Robert Ferrar (or Farrar), D.D., Bishop of St. David's. Burned at Carmarthen.
3. Rev. Dr. Rowland Taylor, Rector of Hadleigh, Suffolk. Burned at Hadleigh.
4. Rev. John Rogers,* Vicar of St. Sepulchre's, and Prebendary of St. Paul's. Burned at Smithfield.
5. The Right Rev. John Hooper, D.D., Bishop of Worcester and Gloucester. Burned at Gloucester.
6. Rev. John Bradford, Prebendary of St. Paul's. Burned at Smithfield.
7. The Ven. John Philpot, B.C.L., Archdeacon of Winchester. Burned at Smithfield.

Toleration was not understood by either side in those days. Take the case of Philpot as an illustration.

Philpot, in his examination, showed that he too could be a persecutor even unto death. It will be remembered that, in the previous reign (Edward VI.), the Reformers condemned to the stake a person named Joan of Kent, for heresy. Philpot, in the course of his trial, declared that "as for Joan of Kent, she was well worthy to be burned."†

Hence it was Philpot's opinion that it was no crime to burn heretics. And it also follows that, had he been in power, he would have sent Gardiner and Bonner, and the rest, to the stake. Whatever party was uppermost considered it quite lawful, in those days, to crush out by torture and death all opposition in the party that was weak and in the minority. Similarly, on the Continent, Calvin consented to the death of Servetus. So also was it in the case of the Pilgrim Fathers, who fled from Europe in search of religious liberty, and scarcely had they touched the shores of New England when they began to persecute each other.

The fifth examination of Merbecke (or Marbecke) was held here in 1543. He was condemned to the stake, but pardoned for the sake of his musical talents.

---

* He was the Editor of the "Thomas Matthew" Bible.

† Foxe, *Book of Martyrs*.

This beautiful Chapel is remarkable, in the third place, as containing the ashes of the erudite and saintly

Bishop Lancelot Andrewes.

HE was born the son of a sea-faring man at Barking, in 1555. He was educated at Merchant Taylors', from which School he proceeded to Pembroke Hall, Cambridge, where, in 1576, he was elected to a Fellowship, and in the following year be became Fellow of Jesus College, Oxford. In 1589 he accepted the living of St. Giles', Cripplegate, and shortly afterwards he was made Prebend of St. Paul's, and Master of Pembroke Hall.

He was a constant preacher at his own church, but was very reluctant to deliver more than one sermon on the same day, remarking that "when he preached twice he prated once."

In 1597 he accepted first a stall, and then the Deanery of Westminster.

Under James I., who was a great admirer of his preaching, his rise was rapid. In 1605, he was persuaded with difficulty to accept the See of Chichester, was translated to the See of Ely in 1609, and in 1619 to the See of Winchester, from which, says Bishop Buckeridge, "God translated him to heaven."

Bishop Andrewes was great (1) as a scholar. He was acquainted with 15 languages, if not more, and Fuller quaintly writes: "The world wanted learning to know how learned this man was, so skilled in all, especially in Oriental languages, that some conceive he might, if then living, almost have served as interpreter-general at the confusion of tongues." It is for this reason, amongst others, that we find his name first on the list of divines appointed in 1607 to frame our Authorised Version of the Bible, the words of which "live on the ear, like music that can never be forgotten, like the sound of church bells, which the wanderer hardly knows how he can forego."

He was president of the Westminster Company of Ten, whose duty it was to translate the Sacred Books from Genesis to the end of Second Kings.

He was great (2) as a preacher. His style fascinated Elizabeth. He was held to be the very *stella prædicantium* (the star of preachers), "a very angel in the pulpit," and that, too, in the palmiest days of English literature.

"Such plagiaries who have stolen his sermons, could never steal his preaching."—(*Fuller*). The late Canon Liddon speaks of him as "a great divine—one of the greatest that Cambridge has ever produced."

He was great (3) as a saint, and possessed the rarest of all gifts, the gift of composing prayers. His "Manual of Private Devotions" has long enjoyed, and still enjoys, an immense popularity, even amongst those who have differed widely from his views. During the last period of his life it was constantly in his hands. "Had you seen," says the first editor of it, "the original MSS., happy in the glorious deformity thereof, being worn with pious hands, and watered with his penitential tears, you would have been forced to confess that book belonged to no other than pure and primitive devotion."

Some authorities have declared that both he and Laud were willing to join the Church of Rome. On the contrary, he wrote* and spoke against her, and went about preaching against her, and made many converts from her to the Church of England. He was distinctly a High Churchman, fond of an elaborate ritual, and had his private Chapels, both at Ely and Winchester. richly adorned. He was tolerant, however, of the views of others, and " content with enjoying without the enjoining."--(*Fuller*).

Can we close without adding that Bishop Andrewes was great (4) as a benefactor of the poor. He left funds and lands for all time, for the benefit of aged poor men, widows, seafaring men, orphans, apprentices, and the promotion of scholars from Free Schools to the University. Most appropriate, therefore, was the text from which Bishop Buckeridge preached his funeral sermon :—

"IN THE PARISH CHURCH OF ST. SAVIORS, IN SOUTHWARKE,

On Saturday, being the XI of Novembre,

A.D. MDCXXVI.

To do good and to distribute forget not: for with such sacrifices God is well pleased. Heb. 13, 16.

A full-length recumbent effigy of the great prelate lies on the tomb, bearing on the left shoulder, engraved on the rich cope, the Cross of St. George and the Garter, with the motto of the Order, *Honi soit qui mal y pense*. The head, covered with a small academical cap, rests on a cushion; the left hand clasps his Manual of Devotions.

---

* Responsio ad Apologiam Cardinalis Bellarmini.

10   TOMB OF BISHOP ANDREWES.

The inscription, which is chiefly taken from an entry in Laud's Diary, states:—

> "On Monday, September 21, in the year 1626, about four o'clock in the morning, Lancelot Andrewes, a most worthy Bishop of Winchester, a light of the Christian world, died.*

A discovery, made six years ago, sent a thrill through the hearts of his admirers – the MS. in Greek, the autograph copy of the Devotions which the Bishop himself used, came to light. It was his dying gift to Laud, afterwards Archbishop of Canterbury, and bears on the outside of the vellum cover the following inscription in Laud's handwriting :—

> "My reverend Friend Bishop Andrewes gave me this Booke a little while before his death.—W : Bath et Welles."

LADYE CHAPEL OR RETRO-CHOIR?

This Ladye Chapel has occasionally been styled within recent times the Retro-Choir; but in the pages of the

---

* Laud makes a mistake in the date; it should be September 25th.

Gentleman's Magazine, where it is constantly referred to from year to year by *eminent architects and antiquaries*, and in all the old books upon St. Saviour's, it invariably receives the charming title of

THE CHAPEL OF OUR LADYE;

by which also it has always been known to the "oldest inhabitant," and by the parishioners from time immemorial; and it is a mere modern affectation to call it by any other name. Dugdale, who is our greatest authority in such matters, also styles it the "Lady Chapel."[*]

For the present it is to be used as the Parish Church. The walls in the interior, from the window-sills to the floor, have had the stucco and plaster removed, and replaced with ashlar; and the groining, which in many places was defective, has been thoroughly repaired. There was a great desire, it would appear, on the part of some, to transfer the tomb of Bishop Andrewes from the west side of this part of the chapel to the south side of the High Altar; but others regarded the monument, containing the ashes and recumbent figure of the saintly prelate, as the only treasure on the parochial side of the Church, and the only solace to the pain and irritation caused by certain offensive inscriptions, which are flaunted in some ugly windows. Here is a choice morsel:—

"Your sacrament of the Mass is no sacrament at all, neither is Christ in any wise present in it."

Another runs as follows:—

"From the Bishop of Rome and all his detestable enormities, good Lord deliver us."

The most uncompromising Anti-Papalist could not surely approve, in his sober moments, words like these, which are so uncharitable, and so insulting to his neighbours and fellow-Christians. These inscriptions are actually driving people to Rome in sheer disgust. A case, within the writer's knowledge, has recently occurred.

---

[*] *Monasticon*, vol. vi., p. 171. See also J. Willis Clark: *The Observances in Use at the Augustinian Priory of Barnwell*, where, in a plan drawn by Mr. St. John Hope, the Lady Chapel occupies a position similar to ours; and jutting out from it at the north-east angle is another Chapel, called the Little Lady Chapel. The true designation of our so-called Bishop's Chapel, which stretched out in an easterly direction through the bay now occupied by the Benson window, until its unfortunate removal in 1830, was, probably, the *Little Lady Chapel*.

A new window, of a different type and style, has been erected here within the last few years. Its place is in the north-east bay, the site of the bench of the ancient Consistorial Court, in honour of St. Thomas à Becket, in whose name the Prior and Canons of St. Mary Overy originally founded the Hospital of St. Thomas, on a site adjoining this Church; and of Charles I., whose name still stands on the roll of benefactors of St. Saviour's as a helper of its poor; and of Archbishop Laud, the disciple and friend of Bishop Andrewes, towards whose shrine he turns his eyes.* This window, also by Kempe, is a masterpiece. The donor is Mrs. Stevenson, in memory of her husband, Captain Curtis William Stevenson, and of her sister Mary.

We now pass down the North Aisle of the Choir, and immediately on the left is the monument of

---

*As to Charles I. His death was illegal. "The execution of Charles I. . . . . the work of military violence cloaked in the merest tatters of legality." This is a candid admission on the part of a great modern historian with a marked Cromwellian bias. Dr. Rawson Gardiner, *History of the Commonwealth*, vol. i., p. 1.

Charles I. was a martyr in the cause of the Church. "Had Charles been willing to abandon the Church, and give up Episcopacy, he might have saved his throne and his life. But on this point Charles stood firm; for this he died, and by dying, saved it for the future." Dr. Creighton, Bishop of London, *Laud Commemoration*, 1895. Lecture 1, p. 25.

As to Becket. Hear his brave utterance, when assailed by his murderers, the four Norman knights: "In vain you menace me; if all the swords in England were brandished over my head, their terrors could not move me. Foot to foot you will find me fighting the battle of the Lord." *Vide* Lord Campbell's *Lives of the Chancellors*.

As to Laud. "That we have our Prayer-Book, our Altar, even our Episcopacy itself, we may, humanly speaking, thank Laud. Laud saved the English Church. The English Church in her Catholic aspect is a memorial of Laud." Dr. Mozley, *Essays*, vol. i., p. 227. *sq.*

Similarly Dr. Creighton. "Laud has an unfailing claim upon the homage of English Churchmen." *Laud Commemoration*, Lecture i., p. 3.

Macaulay's account of Laud is not to be accepted. "The climax" (of abuse of Laud) "was reached in the bitter and strangely distorted estimate of Lord Macaulay." Professor Collins, *ut supra*.

"Macaulay, as usual, is the most rancorous in his abuse." *Times* leader, January 11, 1895.

Laud was the ablest champion of the day against Rome. Read his "Conference with Fisher the Jesuit."

Alderman* Humble.

THIS is a fine Altar Tomb, with kneeling figures, under a canopy, of the Alderman, with his two wives behind him; and basso-relievos of the children on the basement, north and south.

11   TOMB OF ALDERMAN HUMBLE.

* So called. He was duly elected, but he refused the honour, paid the fine, and was 'discharged.'

On the Sanctuary side are inscribed the beautiful and pathetic lines, attributed to Quarles, to Simon Wastell, to Beaumont, and others :—

> "Like to the damask rose you see,
> Or like the blossom on the tree,
> Or like the dainty flower in May,
> Or like the morning of the day,
> Or like the sun, or like the shade,
> Or like the gourd which Jonas had;
> Even so is man, whose thread is spun,
> Drawn out and cut, and so is done!
>
> The rose withers, the blossom blasteth,
> The flower fades, the morning hasteth,
> The sun sets, the shadow flies,
> The gourd consumes, the man he dies.

His daughter married a William Ward, a wealthy citizen and goldsmith of the time, and jeweller to the queen of Charles I. Their son was christened **HUMBLE** Ward, who, after having married Frances, heiress to the Barony of Dudley, was created Baron Ward in 1644, from which union is derived the present house of Dudley and Ward.

The Crusader.

THIS interesting effigy is on the right. It is an exquisite piece of carving in oak, and represents, most likely, one of the de Warrens, Earls of Surrey, who were great Lords of Southwark. He has returned from the last Crusade with Prince Edward of England (the costume is of that period, 1270). As a good soldier of the Cross he has risked his life in defence of the Holy Sepulchre, and now he sheathes his sword, and lies down to rest.

"The strife is o'er, the battle done."

He is clad in chain armour, with a surcoat crossed by

two belts, one for the shield, the other for the sword, and on his head a conical helmet, and a lion at his feet.

Whatever may have been his fortunes in war, he certainly experienced some strange vicissitudes, and suffered many indignities in this Church from time to time. At one period he was tossed about as useless lumber at the west end of the Nave; at another he was placed standing upright close to one of the doors, like a sentinel, " new painted, flourished up, and looking somewhat dreadful "—a device of the enemy, no doubt, to scare and scatter the flock! He was even used as an ordinary prop to support a portion of a stair-case on his head! The marvel is that he exists at all. We are proud to possess him, and to think of him in the days when the banner of the Red Cross was flying in the Holy Land.

12
TREHEARNE MONUMENT. CURE. CRUSADER.

Upon his breast a bloodie Cross he bore,
  The deare remembrance of His dying Lord,
  For whose sweete sake that glorious badge he wore
  And dead, as living, ever Him ador'd;
  Upon his shield the like was also scor'd,
  For soveraine hope which in His helpe he had,
  Right faithful true he was in deede and word,
  But of his cheere did seeme too solemne sad;
Yet nothing did he dread, but ever was ydrad.*—*Spenser.*

Before taking our leave of him we should like to contemplate his attitude in a new light. Amongst the Knights Templars it was the custom, when reciting the Apostles' Creed in their Encampments, to draw the sword about three inches, as in the effigy, in commencing; and at the words, "In Jesus Christ our Lord," to plunge it into the scabbard to the hilt. It will be noticed that the lips are firmly parted. He is saying the *Credo.* He was a believer.

> The Knight's bones are dust,
> And his good sword rust;
> His soul is with the saints, I trust.—*Coleridge.*

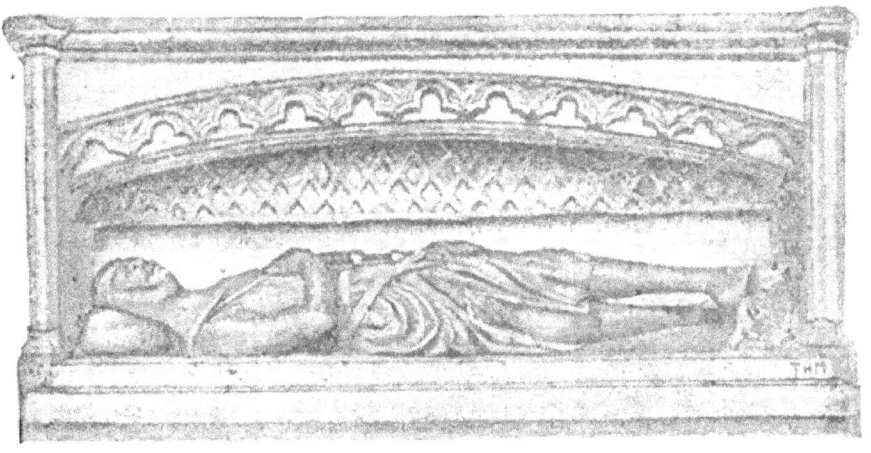

13   Crusader.

---

* Dreaded.

Cure.

IN the corresponding low-arched recess is a plain slab to the memory of the above. He was one of the benefactors of this parish, having been instrumental in founding a " College " for poor people. It would appear, however, that he did not give much out of his own pocket towards the establishment of the " College." The vestry minutes show that he advanced the money to build some houses for the poor, and that the loan was repaid him. The Latin inscription is a punning epitaph on his name :—

> "*Cure*, whom this stone covers, served Elizabeth as master of the saddle horses. He served King Edward and Mary, his sister. It is great praise to have given satisfaction to three sovereigns.
>
> He lived beloved by all.
>
> The State was ever a Care (*Curæ*) to Cure (*Curo*).
>
> The welfare of the people was (a care) to him while he lived.
>
> He cared (*curavit*) and provided that, for the support of the aged, annual gifts of money should be assigned towards the expenses, and houses."

He died on the 24th of May, 1588, thus missing, only by a few days, to share in the rejoicings of the great victory of his Royal Mistress over the Spanish Armada*, which set out from Lisbon on the 29th of that month.

He was thrice M.P. for Southwark.

---

* St. Saviour's Parish provided towards the Armament against the Spaniards, 13 pick-axes, 13 spades, and 13 bills.—*Vestry Minutes*.

Trehearne.

CLOSE to Cure's tablet is a striking monument to John Trehearne and his wife, with the following inscription:—

"AN EPITAPH UPON JOHN TREHEARNE, GENTLEMAN PORTER TO KING JAMES I.

"Had Kings a power to lend their subjects breath,
Trehearne, thou shouldst not be cast down by death;
Thy royal master still would keep thee then,
But length of days is beyond reach of men,
Nor wealth, nor strength, nor great men's love can ease
The wounds death's arrows make, for thou hast these.
In thy king's court good place to thee is given,
Whence thou shalt go to the King's court in heaven."

Now, after the perusal of this eulogy, we should expect better things from him than to find him lax in the payment of his tithes! Here is an extract from the Parish Vestry Minutes, October 15th, 1577:—

"John Trehearne of Bankside pays double for witholding his tythes."

On the shield are *three herons*, in allusion to his name. A *rebus* was a favourite conceit of the times.

Lower down is the Vestry, traditionally known as the Chapel of St. John the Divine.

The North Transept.

WE now enter the North Transept. On the floor, at the right, will be noticed an emaciated effigy in stone. It is simply a *memento mori*, a reminder of mortality. But some would tell you that it was intended to represent

Old John Overs (Overy),

the father of the original foundress of this great Church. He was a rich miser (so the tale runs), who owned a ferry for conveying passengers across the Thames, long before there was any bridge. A strange plan of economizing his household expenses one day entered his mind. He would feign death; for surely, he thought, his family and servants would fast, for one day at least, in their bereavement. On the contrary, it would appear, they were only too happy to be rid of him, and proceeded to feast and make merry over the event. The sound of revelry reaching his ears, he sprang from his bier, and, plunging down stairs in his winding-sheet, threw horror and consternation into the midst of the gay company. A waterman, rushing in his fright and confusion upon what he thought was the ghost of the old man, felled him dead with an oar. Now his daughter, who was "of a beautiful aspect and pious disposition," had a lover, who had not met with the father's approval. The news of the death reaching him in the country, he started with all speed to his sweetheart; but, in his too eager haste, he fell from his horse and was killed. Mary Overs, rendered inconsolable, withdrew from the world and founded a House of Sisters, into which she retired, endowing the institution with the ample profits of her ferry, and dedicating it to the Blessed Virgin Mary.

There is a curious tract, which may be seen in the British Museum, entitled, "*The true History of the Life and sudden Death of old John Overs, the rich Ferry-Man of London, shewing how he lost his Life by his own Covetousness. And of his*

Daughter Mary, who caused the Church of St. Mary Overs in Southwark to be built."

Observe the Royal Coat of Arms, above, of Good Queen Anne. It was painted and set up originally in the choir to commemorate a visit which she paid to the Church to hear the famous preacher, Dr. Henry Sacheverell, a former incumbent of the parish.*

In the north wall is seen an aumbry, or cupboard for books, sacramental vessels, or alms.

---

* He was a High Churchman of the old type, and a Tory, mercilessly maligned by pamphleteers of the opposite school, and hotly defended by those of his own. The sermon, criticising the Whig policy of the hour, which brought him into trouble, was preached in 1709, at St. Paul's Cathedral, before the Lord Mayor, Sir Samuel Garrard, Bart., who urged its publication. By a small majority of the peers before whom the case was tried, he was ordered to cease from preaching for three years, but not debarred from reading Divine Service, or accepting preferment. Retribution instantly followed. His utterances so accurately voiced the feelings of the country that he " upset the administration, altered the foreign policy of the nation, and changed the face of affairs in the whole of Europe " (Perry, *Hist. Ch. Eng.*). The approval of his sermon by the Chief Magistrate of the City of London was, in itself, evidence that the country was actually " In Perils among False Brethren " (the text of the discourse). Sacheverell was a scholar as well as an orator, far-seeing, outspoken. He was a Fellow of Magdalen College, Oxford, and preached before the University, in 1702, a sermon which ran through two editions; and, in the following year at St. Mary's, another, which also reached a second edition; again, before the University in 1707; at Leicester, before the Grand Jury, in the same year; at Derby, in 1709, before the Grand Jury, and his relative, George Sacheverell, High-Sheriff of the County. Almost immediately after the expiration of his suspension he preached at St. Saviour's, in 1713, a fact which shows that his parishioners were still one with him : also in the same year at St. Margaret's, Westminster, before the House of Commons ; and again at St. Paul's, before the Sons of the Clergy, in 1714. With such a solid reputation, and such public confidence as all this implies, his fame and character and worth are safe. He saved the Church from being smothered and strangled by the " Comprehensive Scheme," proposed in his day (and always in the air), which was to include in one heterogeneous body all sorts of religious opinions, self-contradictory, mutually destructive. Churchmen, who have only within the last two or three years woke up to see how much they owe to Laud (p. 31) will one day recognise their indebtedness to Henry Sacheverell. It is almost as true of him as of Laud to say, that, humanly speaking, he saved the Church of England. He died Rector of St. Andrew's, Holborn, a benefice to which he was preferred by Queen Anne, and within its walls he lies buried, in the place of honour, beneath the Altar. *Obiit 5to Junii Anno Domini* 1724.

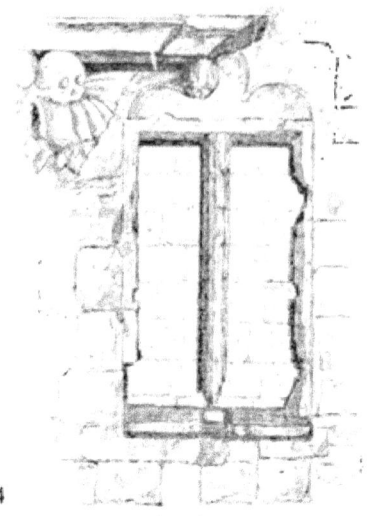
14
Aumbry.

This North Transept, some of the old books inform us, was at one time used as a side chapel, dedicated to St. Peter. The discovery of this aumbry confirms the tradition, for an aumbry always implies a neighbouring altar; and the stilted bases of the great piers on its south side, so unlike the two other corresponding ones, which are moulded to the ground, are now accounted for. A screen was evidently thrown across here.

Underneath is a stone coffin, with a sculptured cross of unique design on its Purbeck-marble lid, in the quarterings of which are representations of the sun, moon, and stars. The date is about 1180.

15

Above will be noticed a window, by Kempe, which may be regarded as illustrating the union of

CHURCH AND STATE.

It is the handsome Diamond Jubilee Gift of Mr. Frederick Lincoln Bevan, in memory of the late Prince Consort, Albert the Good. It was unveiled by H.R.H. the Duke of Connaught, June 22nd, 1898. The subjects are:—

1. Gregory the Great, by whose means Christianity was reinstated in the south-eastern corner of our Island, from which it had been expelled by the Anglo-Saxons, the heathen conquerors of Britain.

2. Ethelbert. He was king of the Kentishmen at that time, and soon became a Convert. His Queen Bertha was already a Christian.

3. Stephen Langton, Cardinal Archbishop of Canterbury, the great Christian patriot, who helped to obtain the *Magna Carta* from King John.

4. William of Wykeham, Bishop of Winchester, Architect, Statesman, and father of the public school system of this country. He was ordained Acolyte, Sub-deacon, and Priest (1362), in the chapel of Winchester House, which adjoined the west end of this Church. (*Reg. Edingdon*, iv. p.p.).

Lockyer.

THE famous pill man—the Holloway of his time. He was an eccentric empiric or quack-doctor in the reign of Charles II., styling himself "Licensed Physician and Chemist," In Manning and Bray's History of Surrey (Guildhall Library copy) there is a picture of him and his Merry Andrew, each on his piebald horse, selling the renowned nostrum in the midst of a large crowd on Tower Hill. In his advertising tract, which is a curiosity in itself, he represents his pills as "extracted from the rays of the sun" (*Pilulæ Radiis Solis Extractæ*). He declares them capable of curing a "Regiment of diseases, known and unknown." "Taken early in the morning, two or three in number, preserves against contagious airs." "They that be well and deserve to be so, let them take the pills once a week." This solar preparation "increases Beauty, and makes old Age comely." In the puffing of his wares he does not scruple to assume the cloak of religion, introducing the Sacred name over and over again. And it will be noted that, consciously or unconsciously, the sculptor has imparted an expression of hypocrisy to the face—its sanctimonious elongation, the downcast eyes, the solemn pose. In all probability it is a faithful likeness.

The inscription :—

> "Here Lockyer lies interr'd; enough, his name
> Speaks one hath few competitors in fame,
> A name so great, so gen'ral, it may scorn
> Inscriptions which do vulgar tombs adorn.
> A diminution 'tis to write in verse
> His eulogies, which most men's mouths rehearse.
> His virtues and his pills are so well known
> That envy can't confine them under stone.
> But they'll survive his dust and not expire
> Till all things else at th' universal fire.
> This verse is lost, his pills embalm him safe
> To future times without an epitaph.
> Deceased, April 26, A.D. 1672. Aged 72.

Londoners especially will regret the total disappearance of this miraculous panacea, inasmuch as it was an antidote against "the mischief of fogs!"

Austin.

THIS monument attracts much attention, and is a Scriptural study in itself. An angel stands on a rock, pointing with the right hand to the sun overhead, with the motto, *Sol Justitiæ*, "The Sun of Righteousness," while in the left there is a sickle. Underneath the angel, on the left and right, are the words, *Vos estis Dei agricultura*, "Ye are God's husbandry." Upon the rock, from which issues a stream, are the words, *Petra erat Christus*, "That Rock was Christ." Close to it is a serpent, whose evil influences were to be neutralized in that fountain of life. Below the rock are sheaves of corn, bound with a scroll, on which are inscribed, *Si non moriatur, non reviviscit*, "It is not quickened except it die." Lower still we read, *Nos sevit, fovit, lavit, cogit, renovabit*, "He hath sown, fostered, and washed us, he gathers us together, and will renew us." On either side there is an angel seated, one with a rake and the other with a pitchfork; beneath one is the word *Congregabunt* "They shall gather," and beneath the other, the word *Messores*, Reapers ("The reapers are the angels"). Lower down is a winnowing fan ("Whose fan is in his hand"), setting forth the family names to whom this burial place (*arcum hoc sepulchrale*) is devoted.

Underneath the monument, on the wall, we find this inflated epitaph: "The resting place of William Austin, Esq., who in contemplation was an angel; in action, a Dædalus; in travel, as good as a conveyance; at table, a feast in himself; in disease, a miracle of patience; in death, a pattern of faith."

He wrote some fugitive pieces of piety; and, on the death of his wife, he compared himself to a tree, half alive, half dead, the "branches withered, cut off, and buried with her." He soon recovered his spirits, however, in finding another better half to supply the place of the half of him that was lost.

On the floor, beneath, is a fine old Muniment Chest of elaborate workmanship, the gift of one Hugh Offley, a Sheriff of London in 1588.

Before leaving this transept, let us look at those

CARVED OAKEN BOSSES,

with their strange devices. We may observe the crown of thorns; "the pelican in her piety" feeding her young from her pierced breast, a well-known mediæval symbol of the "Chalice of the grapes of God" in the Holy Sacrament; a rebus of Henry de Burton (three *burrs* issuing out of a *tun*), who was the Prior when the groined vaulting of wood was set up in the Nave in place of the stone roof which had fallen down in 1469 (Ed. IV.) The quaintest and most extraordinary of all is that flame-coloured face of a fiend swallowing a man. Many conjectures have been made as to its meaning. Most probably it represents Satan swallowing Judas Iscariot, and this view is confirmed by the following lines from Dante's Inferno, canto 34 :—

> " Now this behold . . . .
> For on his head three faces were upreared,
> The one in front of a *vermilion hue :*
> At every mouth his teeth a sinner tore.
> ' That one above,' to me the master said,
> ' Is traitor Judas, doomed to greater pangs ;
> His *feet are quivering*, while *sinks down his head.* "

The New Nave.

"The arborescent look of lofty Gothic aisles."
—Ruskin; *Lamp of Truth*.

Interior View of Nave (looking East).

Let us proceed along the North Aisle. Immediately to the right, as we descend by one step, there was the Prior's doorway, a considerable portion of which still exists on the outer face of this wall, flanked by a damaged *Bénitier* or Holy Water Stoup.

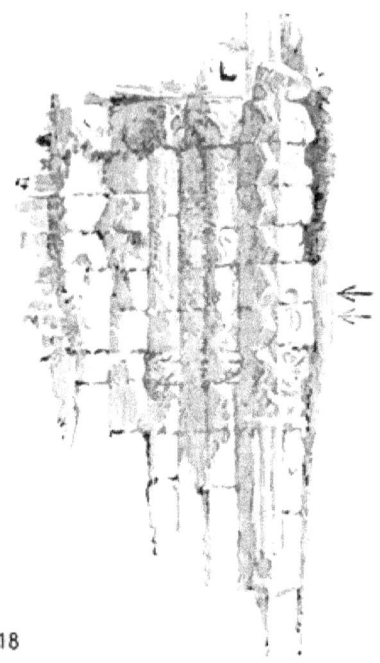

18

Portion of the Prior's Doorway (Norman, 1106) between the Church and the Cloisters, preserved *in situ*, in the new Nave, outside.   Nearly 800 years old.

Note the Consecration Crosses (·) (+) midway on the jamb.

It was a very ancient custom to fix the mark of the Cross on some stone or stones in a Church on the occasion of its completion and consecration, to indicate that both the Church and its site were to be henceforth reserved exclusively for the offices of the Christian religion.

"With the mark of the Cross Churches are dedicated, Altars are consecrated.—(S. AUG. HOM. LXXV. *de Divers*).

The last vestiges of the Cloisters and Priory Buildings, which at one time extended to the river, and from London Bridge to St. Mary Overy's Dock, were swept away about 1835.

A few paces bring us to a monument which would be sufficient of itself to render any church famous.

John Gower.

(1327—1408.)

ST. SAVIOUR'S can boast the unique treasure of the resting-place of the first English poet. Seven cities claimed the honour of the birth-place of the great blind Homer; and similarly more than one spot has coveted a like distinction in respect of our own bard, who was also blind during the eight closing years of his life.

John Gower, it can be easily proved, possessed property and had relatives of his name in Kent; and we believe he was a Kentish man.*

He was Poet Laureate to Richard II. and Henry IV., the latter conferring upon him the SS Collar, with the Lancastrian Badge of the Swan.†

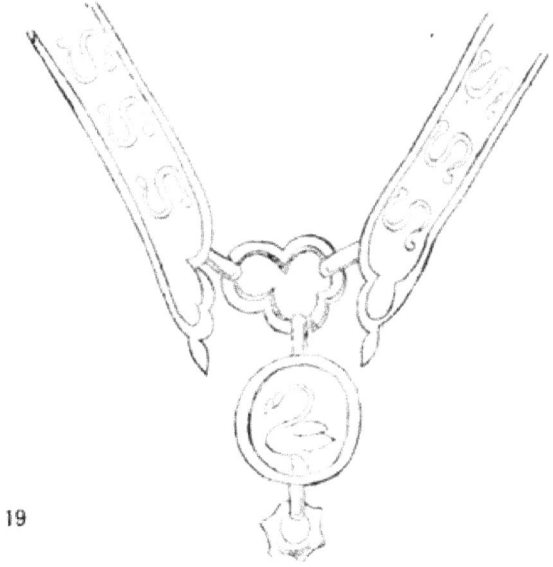

19

---

* *Retrospective Review*, 1828, N.S., vol. ii., pp. 103—117.

† Observe this Collar. There are various interpretations of the "SS." The simplest is that the links of the chain are in the form of the letter S. I incline to think "SS" are the initials of "Silver Swan," the badge of the powerful de Bohun family, who settled in this country soon after the Norman Conquest. When Henry of Bolingbroke, afterwards

20   Tomb of the First English Poet, GOWER.
The above illustration shows the Monument as it was in the South Transept. It is now in its original place.

Henry IV., married Mary de Bohun, he assumed this cognizance of her house. This monarch's tomb in Canterbury is profusely adorned with this favourite device of his, accompanied with the word *Soverayne*, a mistake for *Soveigne*, which is an old form of the French word *Souvenez*. And so a very pretty derivation of the meaning of the S repeated is suggested by the following extract of a warrant *(Wardrobe Accounts in the Office of the Duchy of Lancaster A° 20 Ric.)* " Pro pondere unius Colerii facti cum Esses de Floribus De Soveigne vous De Moy " (Forget-me-nots).

The three large volumes, representing his three principal poetical works, and supporting the head whose brain inspired them, are named *Vox Clamantis*, the "Voice of one Crying," in allusion to the Rebellion of 1381, headed by Wat Tyler and Jack Straw, written in Latin, of which there are several copies extant; *Speculum Meditantis*, the "Mirror of one Meditating," in French, and which has altogether disappeared; and the *Confessio Amantis*, the "Confession of a Lover," in English, and now published in a cheap form. The whole tendency of these great works was to improve the morals and manners of his age, and hence he is styled "Moral Gower" by his fellow-poet, friend, and pupil, Chaucer.

He entered the state of matrimony when he was more than seventy years old, and retired for the rest of his days, with Agnes Groundolf, his wife, within the precincts of the Priory, and contributed largely from his ample means to the repairs of the fabric, founded a chantry in the Chapel of St. John the Baptist, which stood in the fifth bay from the west of the North Aisle of the Nave; in which shrine at last he was buried, and where over his remains the Priors erected this fine monument.

The tomb is in the Perpendicular, or Third-Pointed order of architecture, the style of the period, and consists of a canopy of three arches embellished with cinquefoil tracery, etc., and supported on either side by angular buttresses surmounted with carved pinnacles. Between these three arches are two columns terminating in similar carved pinnacles, and further back and above is a screen composed of two rows of trefoil niches. Against the wall, in the spaces, covered until recently with *Old French* inscriptions, were formerly three painted niches, which were occupied by figures of three Virgins, *Charity*, *Mercy*, *Pity*, crowned with ducal coronets; and with golden scrolls, bearing the following legends, entwining their forms :—

    1. En toi qui filtz de Dieu le pere,
       Sauve soit qui gist soubs ceste pierre.

    2. O bon Jesu, fait ta mercie
       A lalme dont le corps gist icy.

    3. Pour ta pitie Jesu regarde,
       Et met ceste alme en sauve garde.

We submit the following translation:—

1. Thro' Thee, the Father's Only Son,
   Be safe who lies beneath this stone.

2. Thy mercy, O Good Jesu, show
   The soul, whose body lies below.

3. For pity's sake, O Jesu, keep
   The soul of him who here doth sleep.

An ingenious rendering of the Latin lines (*Armigeri scutum, &c.*), once beneath the place of the Virgins, is given by the late Prof. Henry Morley* :—

"No squire's shield defending will guard you from this way of ending;
He has paid the unbending Death's tax over all men impending;
Glad be the soul's wending, no more with the flesh interblending,
'Tis where, God amending, the Virtues reign free from offending."

On the ledge of the tomb we read (*Hic jacet, &c.*), "Here lies J. Gower, Esq., a most celebrated English Poet, and to this sacred building a distinguished benefactor. He lived in the times of Ed. III., Ric. II. and Heni IV."

It is earnestly to be hoped that some generous friend will take this noble monument in hand, restore all the old inscriptions back to their places, and provide the window above with painted glass.

Further down we reach two Norman relics. The first is the Canons' doorway, quite plain in its moulding, and forming in this respect a striking contrast with the rich ornamentation of the doorway of their Chief (p. 46).† The threshold, it will be seen, is three feet below the level of the floor of its Early English successor, and led into the Cloisters by one or two descending steps. The other is a recess which was, perhaps, originally occupied by a recumbent figure. It has been suggested that

---

* English Writers, Vol. iv., p. 161.

† These two doors are to be opened into the New Vestries, which, it is hoped, will soon be erected on the north side of the Nave, on a site at present occupied by stables.

21
CANONS' NORMAN DOORWAY.

it must have belonged to our Knight Templar; but there are two fatal objections to this view. In the first place, he was not of the Norman period, as the armour clearly shows; and secondly, the recess is not of sufficient length to accommodate him.

22 NORMAN RECESS

Stepping aside into the Nave, we have a good view of the

West Window.

IT is a memorial window, by Holliday, the gorgeous[*] gift of Mr. H. T. Withers, and has cost over £600. It is of the Burne-Jones type, and is intended to represent Christ as the "Creator Mundi," as its counterpart in the east is designed to set forth Christ as the "Salvator Mundi."

In the upper part of the central light, Christ is seated, enthroned as "Creator Mundi." In His hand is the Universe, and above and around Him are adoring Seraphim, and on either side are the words, "Let the Heavens rejoice and the Earth be glad." In the heads of the two side lights are cherubim with scrolls bearing the words, "Holy, Holy, Holy, Lord God of Hosts."

In the centre part of the three lights are represented the six Days of Creation, each day enclosed in a circle. Under each circle is a panel illustrating one or more verses of the hymn, "Benedicite, Omnia Opera," bearing upon the subject of that day's creation. At the base of the centre light appear the three holy children in the furnace—Ananias, Azarias, and Misael—to whom is attributed the beautiful Song, and in the side lights are saints noted for their hymns of praise—David and Deborah, Miriam and Moses (the historian of the Creation).

Moving to the left, we notice, to the right of the porch, a considerable fragment, preserved *in situ*, of Early English arcading—a weather-beaten relic, not only of interest, but of use, as giving the key to the treatment of the lower portion of the west wall.

This bay, being close to the main entrance, is to form the Baptistery, for which a Font is promised by Mr. Alfred H. Bevan; and in its two pictured windows, by Kempe, an attempt is made to show the connection of St. Saviour's with its former and present diocese, the subject of one window being St. Swithun, coped and mitred, blessing his cathedral of Winchester, and of the other St. Paulinus, third Bishop of

---

[*] It glows and burns like a bonfire when the summer sun approaches the west. It is not fair to pass an opinion on this or any window, unless seen in its proper light.

23   EARLY ENGLISH ARCADING (1207).

Rochester, baptising a host of Saxon warriors in a river. The picture of the saint in the lowest panel has, surely, never been excelled. The introduction of the figure of the former saint is doubly appropriate from the fact that it was he who first made St. Mary Overy a Collegiate Church, by converting a House of Sisters, which was the original establishment, into a College of Priests. The present Collegiate Body, therefore, though so recently formed, may well lay claim to a high ancestry. The first window is the gift of Mr. J. F. Field; and the second, to the memory of Mr. J. Norwood, a late Rector's warden, has been provided by his friends in the parish.

It was at this door* Edmond Holland, Earl of Kent, received the hand of the daughter of the Duke of Milan. "The King (Henry IV.) was there himselfe, and gafe hir at the church dore. And when they were y-wedded, and masse was done, the kyng his owne persone brought and led this

---

* There was no western doorway before the middle of the 15th century, and, perhaps, not until after the fall of the nave roof in 1469.

worthy lady into the bishoppes place of Wynchester, and there was a wonder grete fest y-holden to all manner of people that comen."*

It was here that James I. of Scotland (p. 12) received his Lady Joan Beaufort, in " her golden hair and rich attire," who, sometime previously, while walking with her maidens in "a garden fair fast by the tower's wall" of his Windsor prison, seemed to him like " God Cupid's own princess," and as

" The fairest or the freshest youngé flower
That ever I saw, methought, before that hour";

and in whom

" There was, well I wot,
Beauty enough to make a world to doat."†

At the conclusion of the nuptial ceremony, " They kept their marriage feast in the bishoppe of Winchester's place, by the sayde church of St. Mary Overies."‡

We have now arrived at the principal entrance—

The South-West Porch.

LADY COBHAM, more than five hundred years ago, towards the close of the reign of Edward III., gave directions in her will that her body should be buried in front of it, " where the image of the Blessed Virgin sitteth on high over that door"; and that a marble slab, bearing a metal cross, should be laid upon her grave, with the following inscription :—

" *Vous qui per ici passietz pur l'alme Johane de Cobham prietz.*"

A little group of statuary in the vacant niches in the porch outside, above the door, would remove the present sense of incompletion, and be an appropriate enrichment.

Proceeding up the south aisle, we meet with a remarkable series of windows—all by Kempe. Southwark is classic

---

* Caxton: *Cronycles of Eng.*, 1482.

† *The King's Quair*, the charming love-poem which he composed in her honour in the days of his exile. It consists of 200 stanzas of seven lines each. *Quair* signifies *Book: c.f. quire* (of paper).

‡ Stow: *Annals*.

ground, and around and within its great Church cluster literary associations which are unique and of the deepest interest. Bankside is famous as the scene of the almost sudden outburst of dramatic genius in the days of Elizabeth. Let us commence with the first in order and size in this striking dramatic series. It is the gift of Sir Frederick Wigan, Bart., in honour of William Shakespeare, and in memory of a brother-in-law, the late well-known Arthur Cecil Blunt. This window is a triplet, and contains in the central light a representation of the Muse of Poetry enthroned, and on the steps to right and left stand, as supporters, the figures of Shakespeare and Spenser. The face of Edmond Shakespeare, the poet's brother, who is buried in the church, is introduced into one of the quatrefoil openings in the head of the window, and that of A. C. Blunt in another; and over that of the Muse is the Dove, the symbol of the Spirit of God, and of the inspiration of the Almighty, the source of all that is good in literature, as in everything else; and at the base are the words, " Doctrix disciplinæ Dei, et electrix operum illius" (*Wisdom* viii. 4).

The Massinger window comes next.

The subject is taken from his *Virgin Martyr*. St. Dorothea* occupies the lowest panel; a scene after her martyrdom is represented in the middle of the window, and the upper part shows the medallion portrait of the author. The cost of this window was guaranteed by the Rector, and was the first of the series erected. The following list of names indicates the widespread interest taken in the movement.

SUBSCRIBERS:

The Duke of Westminster, The Marquis of Ripon, Lord

---

* She was a young girl of Cappadocia, who was martyred in the days of Diocletian. On her way to execution an unbelieving lawyer requested her, in mockery, to send him some apples and roses from the Paradise, to which she said she was hastening. The legend goes on to say that the apples and roses were sent, although the ground at the time lay deep in snow. The lawyer in his study exclaims in wonder;—
 "What flowers are these!
 Frost, ice and snow hang on the beard of winter;
 Where's the sun that gilds this summer?"
His conversion to the faith he despised and persecuted immediately followed. It is this visit of *Angelo* which is represented in the middle panel.

Kinnaird, The Bishop of Bristol, Sir Frederick Leighton, Sir Walter Besant, Sir Henry Doulton, Sir Henry Irving; Professors Hales, Ker, Sainsbury, Shuttleworth, Skeat, and Sylvester; Messrs. Beerbohm Tree, R. Le Gallienne, Stanley

24

Weyman, Forbes Robertson, Arthur W. Pinero, Wilson Barrett, J. B. Bancroft, Henry James, Percy M. Thornton, M.P., E. Gosse, Sidney Lee, Joseph Knight, W. M. Rossetti, Canon Benham, Mrs. Lynn Lynton, Miss Braddon, Mrs. Richard Hunt, Mrs. Hugh Lonsey, the Rector, and others.

The window to John Fletcher, who lies buried in the same grave with Massinger in the church, soon followed, his *Knight of Malta* furnishing the theme. At the base is figured St. John the Baptist, the patron saint of the Knights of St. John, carrying the staff and banner of the Lamb, from which a streamer floats, bearing the words *Pour la Foy*, the motto of the order: the investiture of a knight by two Bishops, with many attendants, before the altar, is shown in the second panel; and surmounting all is the head of the dramatist entwined with bay. It is the gift of the family of Mr. T. F. Rider, the builder of the Nave.

With regard to his colleague, Francis Beaumont, his writings are so inextricably entangled with those of Fletcher that it was found impossible to obtain suitable subjects from them. Friendship was therefore chosen as the theme. The central panel represents David with his harp and Jonathan with his bow, seated beside a stand, upon which rests the Book of the Psalms, open at the words:—" Ecce quam bonum et jucundum habitare fratres in unum " (Ps. cxxxiii. 1); below is the figure of *Concordia*, with the family shields of the two poets conjoined in the base. The uppermost panel contains the portrait of Beaumont. The donor is Mr. W. H. Francis, the Rector's warden.

The next window, which terminates this unique series, is to Edward Alleyne, who was one of the chief exponents of the drama in the days of the foregoing writers. As an actor he was second only to Burbage. He was one of the Corporation of Wardens of St. Saviour's in 1610, but he is best known as the founder of the " Colledge of God's Guift " in Dulwich in 1619. In the lowest panel is a figure of Charity holding a banner in her left hand, upon which is depicted a flaming heart, and, with her right hand extended, she invites little children in the words on the encircling scroll, " Come, ye children, hearken unto me: I will teach you the fear of the Lord " (Ps. xxxiv., 11). In the middle panel Alleyne is seen reading, in the College Chapel, the charter and constitution of his foundation, in the presence of Lord Chancellor Bacon, Lord Arundel, Inigo Jones, and others. His portrait occupies the head of the window. The Chancellor said, " I like well that Alleyne playeth the last act of his life so well."

This memorial has been provided by the Governors, Old Scholars, and friends of the College.

It was unveiled by H.R.H. the Duke of Connaught, June 22nd, 1898.

The Grand Candelabra.

RETURNING to the South Transept, and standing well back, beneath the "Jesse Tree," and looking north, we have a good view of both Transepts, the graceful arches and solid pillars of the Tower, and the handsome Candelabra. This last, the gift of Dorothy Applebee in 1680, is one of the finest and most beautiful of its kind to be found anywhere.

North Transept. Candelabra. Part of Choir (before the introduction of the Canopied Stalls).

The New Lectern.

IT is of bronze, solid and graceful, and over six feet in height. There we see a strong majestic eagle firmly grasping in his claws the writhing form of a dragon; a group which symbolises the might of Truth, or the Word of God, strangling the spirit of lies, or the power of evil. It is the gift of Mrs. Richard Hunt in memory of her husband, and contains an inscription to which the letters R.I.P. are appended.

Choir and Altar Screen.

WE now take our stand beneath the Tower, and before us is a full view of the Choir, one of the most chaste and perfect examples of Early English work, with Triforium, Clerestory, and groined stone roof, terminated with a magnificent Altar screen, the gift of Bishop Fox, in 1520. Shortly before this he had bestowed a similar gift upon his own Cathedral at Winchester. Both screens agree in several particulars, not only in the arrangement and general design, but in the actual number of the niches.* Perhaps the present

---

* So wrote an eminent archæologist (*Gent's. Mag.* 1834, Pt. I., pp. 151-4.
 The present aspect of the Winchester screen, in its recent happy and successful restoration, rich in noble statuary of force and feeling and true artistic merit, does not seem to confirm the opinion as to equality in the number of niches. It, too, has suffered much in its time at the hands of "classical" enthusiasts; the fronts of canopies and pedestals were hacked away to provide a smooth and level surface for a wooden Baldacchino, and clumsy urns on ugly bases—senseless and incongruous ornaments—were introduced (*Vide* Dean Kitchin's *Great Screen of Winchester Cathedral*).

 Our own GREAT SCREEN became the victim of similar barbarous treatment, in the days when a wooden substitute, the supposed design of Wren, with pictured urns and all the rest, was raised against it, so as to completely hide it!

number (33) was chosen in allusion to the thirty-three years of our Lord's earthly life. This costly legacy is stamped with

26 THE CHOIR.
(Taken before removal of Candelabra to its original position beneath the Tower).

Fox's peculiar device, the Pelican feeding her young. The same device, however, we have already pointed out on one of the bosses belonging to the roof of the Nave, which was rebuilt fifty years before, and which, therefore, could not have been the work of this Bishop. It contains one or two grotesques, from which the one at Winchester is free, probably, it is said, because the latter was wrought more immediately under his own eye, but, as a matter of fact, we find him very frequently residing at his Southwark palace at this period. Carvers in those days were allowed to indulge their eccentricities a little too freely. Here we have a man chasing a *fox*—a rude mode, very likely, on the part of the workman, of connecting the Bishop's name with his gift.* The Screen, which is about 30 feet in height, is divided horizontally, as in the Winchester example, into three stages or stories. Vertically it is also tripartite. This arrangement was adopted in allusion to the sacred number Three. The most important variations from its original design, for which Wallace, the architect, who restored it in 1833, is responsible, consist in the addition of the cornices, filled with angels, above the lowest and second stories; and over the third, the range of angels holding shields. But the most significant change was the introduction of niches in the middle space of the lowest stage, behind the High Altar. This space, which seems to have been an exact square, was left entirely blank by Fox, with the exception of two small niches, one on each side close to the ogee-headed doors. The Winchester Screen possessed this same peculiarity. The blank was evidently intended by the Bishop to be occupied by some work of art in painting, sculpture, or mosaic. And when we proceed to fill the niches with statues, a work which will no doubt be soon taken in hand, it would be only fair to the memory of the munificent prelate, who has left us this valuable legacy, to return to his original design. The corresponding space in Winchester Cathedral is now filled with Benjamin West's picture of the Raising of Lazarus. At present our Screen is like a picture-frame without the picture— a scene of magnificent emptiness! But when the niches are filled up with appropriate statues, what a resplendent spectacle we shall have in this Choir—an assemblage of angels, and saintly men of the past, prophets and apostles, uniting, as it were, in the glorious anthem, *Te Deum Laudamus.* The ancient materials of the Screen consist of Caen and firestone. Painswick stone was used in its restoration. Such portions as are new were scrupulously worked from models made from the original remains, and replaced in the same situations which were occupied by the originals.

---

* The introduction of this device would not, however, have been displeasing to the Bishop; for we learn that when President of Pembroke Hall, Cambridge, he "gave hangings thereunto with a Fox woven therein."

William Wickham ii., Bishop of Winchester, lies buried (1595) within the Sacrarium, without a line or word on any stone to indicate the spot. They have not treated him so at Winchester, although their recognition has been tardy. And on the floor of the Choir are names to conjure with— Edmond Shakespeare (1607), John Fletcher (1625), and Philip Massinger (1639).*

This is all the notice that has been taken of them for centuries. The first was:—

> ". . . . . a poor player,
> Who struts and frets his hour upon the stage,
> And then is heard no more."

And yet he was the brother of the immortal "Swan of Avon," the poet "not of an age, but of all time," and our most distinguished PARISHIONER, who lived, and wrote some of the most magnificent of his masterpieces, in this Parish, for representation at "the most celebrated theatre the world has ever seen" (Halliwell-Phillips), in which our Poet held shares— the Globe of Bankside; the site of which, at present covered by the brewery of Messrs. Barclay, Perkins & Co., is close at hand. It was in this Parish the genius of William Shakespeare rose to its greatest height. Shortly after the death of Edmond, he retired for the rest of his brief days to his native town, which, if we may trust tradition, he never failed to visit annually from the time he left it to seek his fortune on the London boards. In 1616, on his 52nd birthday (St. George's Day, April 23rd), he passed into that "undiscovered country from whose bourne no traveller returns."

To the other two belonged also the poet's pen:—

> ". . . . . the true divining rod
> Which trembles towards the inner founts of feeling."

Let Fletcher, a Bishop's son, remind us, in his own words, of this one useful lesson:—

> "Our acts our angels are, or good or ill,
> Our fatal shadows that walk by us still."

And as to Massinger, the note of his burial in our church

---

* The inscriptions are mere modern scratches. These men, and some of their fellow-poets and actors, have recently been honoured, as we have seen, with memorial windows in the Nave.

register 'implores the passing tribute of a sigh.'—" Philip Massinger, stranger." Here the word "stranger" does not simply signify that he was not a parishioner, but that he died in poverty and obscurity He had lived in great distress, and would have perished from sheer want, but for the bounty of one or two men of rank. He lived in this parish, he and Fletcher occupying one room between them on Bankside.

He had instructed others in " The New Way to Pay Old Debts," but he himself, poor fellow, had to trust for his own discharge to that Old, Old Way through the Valley of the Shadow, wherein all human claims are cancelled, and the burden of penury is laid down.

Gifts and Donors.

IT will, perhaps, be convenient here, as most of them are in sight, to enumerate (*pour encourager les autres*) some of the gifts which the Church has received during its Restoration and since :—

Gifts.	Donors.
The Organ	Mrs. Robert Courage.
Pulpit	Miss Nottidge.
Bronze Eagle Lectern	Mrs. Richard Hunt.
Chancel wrought-iron Screen	Mr. Barclay.
Six Canopied Stalls	Diocese of Rochester, in memory of Bishop Thorold's Episcopate.
Choir Stalls	Anon., per Dr. Talbot, our present Bishop.
Chancel Carved Oak Screens, North and South sides	Sir Fredk. Wigan, Bart.
Bronze Altar Rails	Mr. Norbury Pott
Glastonbury Chair	Mrs. Boger.
High Altar	Mr. J. F. France.
Chalice and Paten, silver-gilt	Canon Bristow.
Altar Cross, silver parcel-gilt	Mr. A. M. Broadley.
Altar Candlesticks, silver	Mrs. Barrow.
Altar Vases, silver	Mr. H. C. Richards, M.P.

*East Window	Sir Fredk. Wigan, Bart.
Processional Cross, silver gilt	Mr. Marson.
Alms Dish, richly gilt and embossed	Mrs. Curtis W. Stevenson.
Vergers' silver Wands ...	Mr. Brankston.
Cope	Rev. C. E. Brooke.
Embroidery Work	Lady Barbara Yeatman, Hon. Mrs. Talbot, Miss Barrow, and others.
Books, mounted in silver and jewelled	Mrs. Huxtable, and the Grey Ladies.
†Tower Clock and Chimes ...	Sir Fredk. Wigan, Bart.
Charles I., Becket and Laud Window, in the Ladye Chapel	Mrs. Curtis W. Stevenson
Prince Consort Window in North Transept	Mr. Fredk. Lincoln Bevan.
West Window	Mr. H. T. Withers.
St. Swithun Window ...	Mr. J. F. Field.
St. Paulinus Window ...	Friends of the late Mr. John Norwood.
Edw. Alleyne Window ...	Governors and Old Scholars of Dulwich College, and Friends.
Beaumont Window	Mr. W. H. Francis.
Fletcher Window	Mr. T. F. Rider's Family.
Massinger Window	Literary People, chiefly.
Shakespeare Window ...	Sir Fredk. Wigan, Bart.
Newcomen Window in South Transept	Governors, Old Scholars and Parishioners.
South Transept Window ...	Sir Fredk. Wigan, Bart.

---

* A memorial to his grandson. The subject is the Crucifixion. The blue sky in the background of the figure on the right of the spectator is "powdered" with the letter I. crowned, for St. John; and that on the left with M crowned, for the Blessed Virgin Mary. The meaning of the dossal, which falls behind the Cross, is obvious from an artistic point of view. Considered symbolically, it represents the veil by which the Mystery of Atonement is concealed from the outside world. To understand that Mystery it is necessary to come within the Church, and when we enter, this curtain becomes a Robe of Estate, reminding us that we are in the presence, not of a malefactor, but of a Monarch, even the Son of God, King of Kings. In this window Kempe departs from his wonted style. The amber canopy is quite out of the common, and is preferable, for once at least, to the usual forest of silver shafts and pinnacles. Time will soon tone down the exuberant richness of the gold.

† Set going by H.R.H. the Duke of Connaught, June 22nd, 1898.

GIFTS NEEDED.

	£	s.	d.
Restoration Fund (*urgent*) about	6,000	0	0
Choir Vestry Building, and Cost of Site (*urgent*)	3,000	0	0
Repairs to Tower (externally and internally)	300	0	0
Restoration of Choir (externally)	1,665	0	0
Repairs to Boundary Walls and Railings	1,000	0	0
Painted Glass Windows, each from	75	0	0
Figures for Altar Screen „ „	80	0	0
Sanctuary Standard Lights, each	50	0	0

Many other needs might be mentioned, but we would draw special attention to those marked "urgent."

Reopening Ceremony.

"*Brothers, to-day's occasion is without parallel in the history of England.*"—Bishop of Winchester's *Sermon*.

AFTER seven years' labour bestowed upon it, and £50,000,* our restored Church was re-opened on February 16th, 1897, in the presence of Their Royal Highnesses the Prince of Wales, the Duke of Teck, and the late greatly loved and lamented Princess Mary, the Archbishop of Canterbury, the Bishops of Rochester and Southwark, and a large number of prelates and dignitaries, the Lord Mayor and Sheriffs, and a vast congregation. The processional Psalms were the 84th, the 122nd, and the 150th. The chief musical feature of the service was the *Te Deum*, sung to Stanford in B flat. The prayers and thanksgiving were read by the Bishop of the Diocese, and by the Rector. The Bishop of Winchester preached the sermon. Archbishop Temple pronounced the benediction. "Now thank we all our God," was the recessional hymn.

* The amount expended on the work has now reached £80,000, to the great benefit (to take the lowest view of the matter) of trade and the working-man.

Thus concluded a service which will stand out prominently, even in the long majestic history of St. Mary Overie. The ceremony was imposing and impressive, and worthy of inaugurating a fresh epoch in her life, and launching her on a new career of wider and more varied influence and usefulness, it is hoped, than ever marked any previous period of her existence.

The New Chapter.

At 8.30 a.m. on the same day, prior to the celebration of the Holy Communion, the installation of the following members of the Chapter took place:—

The Bishop of Rochester (acting as)	Dean.
The Bishop of Southwark "	Sub-dean.

Four Canons.

Canon Thompson, D.D., Rector	Chancellor.
Canon Taylor, M.A.	Precentor.
Canon Rhodes Bristow, M.A.	Missioner.
Canon Allen Edwards, M.A.	Lecturer.

Four Laymen.

Sir Fredk. Wigan, Bart.	Treasurer.
Mr. J. F. Field	Assistant Treasurer.
The Warden of the Great Account } The Rector's Warden }	Ex-Officio.

Mr. Henry Langston	Chapter Clerk.

Rev. E. C. Philpott, M.A.	Succentor.
Dr. Madeley Richardson, M.A., Mus. Doc.	Organist.

The Priors* of St. Marie of Suthewercha.

27
SEAL OF THE PRIORY.

1	Aldgod or Aldgood		...	1106 to 1130
2	Algar	... ...	...	1130 „ 1132
3	Warin	. ...	...	1132 „ 1142

* Taken from *Regist. Priorat. in Bibl. Cotton. Faustina, A.S.*, and other sources.

4	Gregory	1142 to 1150
5	Ralph	1150 „ 1154
6	Richard	1154 „ 1163
7	Valerianus	1163 „ 1189
8	William de Oxenford	1189 „ 1203
9	Richard de St. Mildred	1203 „ 1205
10	William Fitz Samari	1205 „ 1206
11	Martin	1206 „ 1218
12	Robert de Oseney	1218 „ 1223
13	Humphrey	1223 „ 1240
14	Eustachius	1240 „ 1253
15	Stephen	1253 „ 1266
16	Alan	1266 „ 1283
17	William Wallys	1283 „ 1306
18	Peter de Cheyham	1306 „ 1326
19	Thomas de Southwark	1326 „ 1331
20	Robert de Welles	1331 „ 1348
21	John de Peckham	1348 „ 1359
22	Henry Collingbourne	1359 „ 1395
23	John Kyngeston	1395 „ 1397
24	Robert Weston	1397 „ 1414
25	Henry Werkeworth	1414 „ 1452
26	John Bottisham	1452 „ 1462
27	Henry de Burton	1462 „ 1486
28	Richard Briggs	1486 „ 1491
29	John Reculver	1491 „ 1499
30	Richard Michell	1499 „ 1512
31	Robert Shouldham	1512 „ 1513
32	Bartholomew Linstede *alias* Fowle	1513 „ 1540

Linstede surrendered the Priory to Henry VIII. in 1540, and received a pension of £100 a year, and a residence in the Precincts.

LIST OF THE CHAPLAINS.*

The Church was usually served by two "Preaching Chaplains" of independent powers, until recent years, when, by Act 31 Vic., 1868, both were merged in one, and by Act 46-7 Vic., 1883, the last of the Chaplains became the first Rector.

Rev.				Rev.		
	Kelle	...	1564		Dr. Wm. Hoare	1678
"	James Hollyland		1564	"	Dr. Samuel Barton	1687
"	Harman	...	1565	"	**Dr. H. SACHEVERELL**	1705
"	Styles	...	1578	"	Thomas Horne...	1709
"	Smythe...	...	1582	"	Wainford	1724
"	Pattersle	...	1585	"	Dr. Benj. Slocock	1725
"	Hansonne	...	1585	"	John Smith, M.A.	1729
"	Redcliffe..	...	1585	"	Thos. Jones, M.A.	1753
"	M. Ed. Philips...		1589	"	Wm. Day, M.A.	1762
"	Butterton	...	1599	"	Sambrook Russell	1768
"	Marberry	...	1601	"	Philip Batteson..	1769
"	Currie	...	1603	"	W. Winkworth,	
"	Knapp	...	1604		M.A.	1794
"	Snape .		1604	"	W. Mann, M.A.	1804
"	Church...	...	1605	"	Thomas Bird ...	1807
"	Symonds	...	1605	"	Dr. W. Harrison	1808
"	Francis...	...	1606	"	W. Curling, M.A.	1833
"	James Archar ...		1614	"	S. Benson, M.A.	1843
"	Dr. Thos. Sutton		1615	"	Dr. W. Thompson,	
"	Harris ...	...	1623		Curate... ...	1879
"	P. Micklethwaite		1625		Sole Chaplain ...	1881
"	Nicolas Morton..		1627		Rector	1885
"	Robert Knightly		1656†		Canon & Chancellor	1897

* Chiefly derived from the Vestry Minutes, which commence in 1557, and from the Church Registers. Amongst the Ashburnham MSS., now in the *Brit. Mus.*, is one of our old Registers. In the *Ninth Report Hist. MSS. Comm.* (Part iii), p. 29a, it is thus described, in 1881: "The Parochial Register of St. Mary Overy, in Southwark. A folio bound in oak, with brass bosses on the sides. The Register consists of 682 pages in one hand, of the reign of Henry VIII., and before the suppression of monasteries." It is in Latin.

† Church Register. The Vestry Book from 1628 to 1670 is missing. In an entry in the College of Arms we read of one Meriwether marrying, in 1687, "Susanna daughter of Stephen Watkins of the Borough of Southwark sometime Minister of St. Mary Overies Church." Watkins would fit in with the period covered by the lost Vestry Book. Note how the old name clings to the Church.

28

Exterior View from South-east, showing door of South Aisle of Choir, Organ Chamber, and part of South Transept with new doorway.

This angle was the site of the Chapel of St. Mary Magdalene, built by Peter de Rupibus, in the 13th century, for use as a Parish Church. It was removed in 1822, on the occasion of the restoration of the Choir.

Note fast disappearing *matrix* of a brass, marking its South-eastern corner.

The new Organ Chamber occupies a portion of this site.

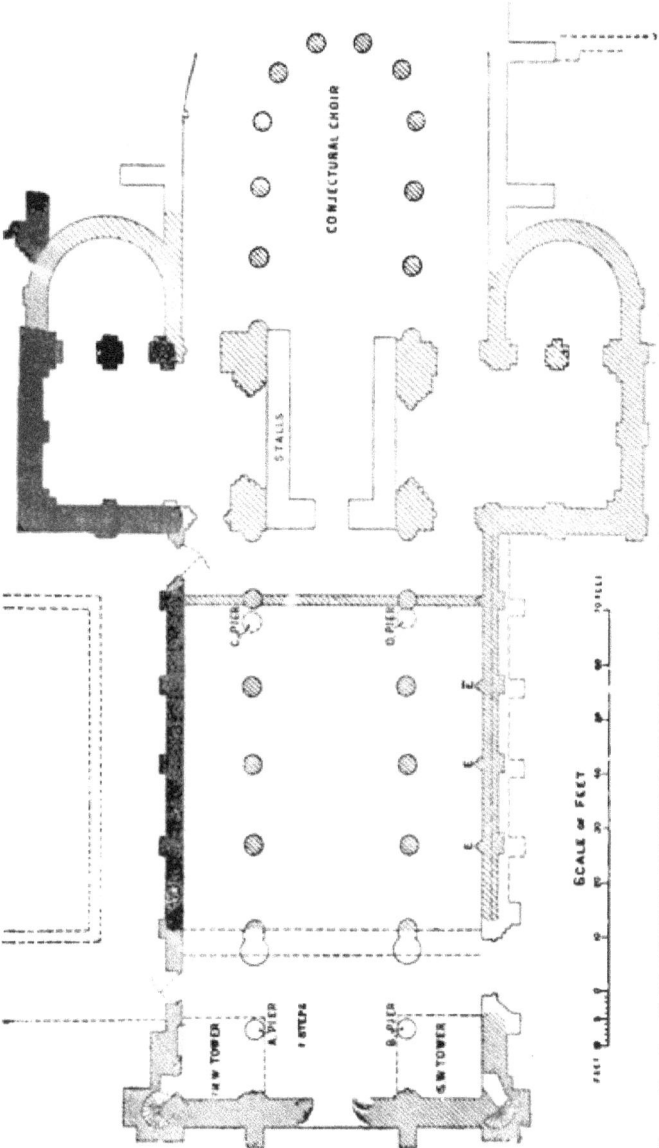

Fig. 1.—PLAN SHOWING SUGGESTED ADAPTATION OF THE EARLY NORMAN CHURCH FOR THE AUGUSTINE CANONS, WITH THE ALTERATIONS AND ADDITIONS.

A, B, C, D, Early English Piers. E E E, Existing Bases. The dotted lines across the Nave show the conjectural west wall of the Early Norman Church.

ARCHITECTURAL STYLES IN ST. SAVIOUR'S.

Sample.	Name of Style.	Date.	Reigning Sovereigns.	
Remains of Saxon Apse,* north side of Sacristy.	Anglo Norman. Early Norman.	1066—1140 (about)	William I. William II.	Henry I. Stephen.
Remains of Prior's doorway, Canons' doorway, and recess in Nave, and parts of North Transept.	Transition between Norman and Early English. Late Norman	1140—1189 (about)		Stephen. Henry II.
Choir, Ladye Chapel, and Nave.	Early English. By some called 13th Century work.	1189—1260 (about)	Richard I. John.	Henry III.
Portions of Ladye Chapel.	Transition between Early English and Decorated.	1260—1300 (about)		Henry III. Edward I.
Transepts and first stage of Tower.	Decorated, also known as Geometrical.	1300—1350 (about)	Edward I. Edward II.	Edward III.
South Transept, very late decorated.	Transition between Decorated and Perpendicular.	1350—1399 (about)		Edward III. Richard II.
Screen and two upper stages of Tower.	Perpendicular.	1399—1547 (about)	Henry IV. Henry V. Henry VI. Edward IV.	Edward V. Henry VII. Henry VIII
Happily all swept away.	Renaissance.	1547—1600 (about)	Edward VI. Mary.	Elizabeth.

* Vide Dollman, *Priory of St. Mary Overie*, p. 23

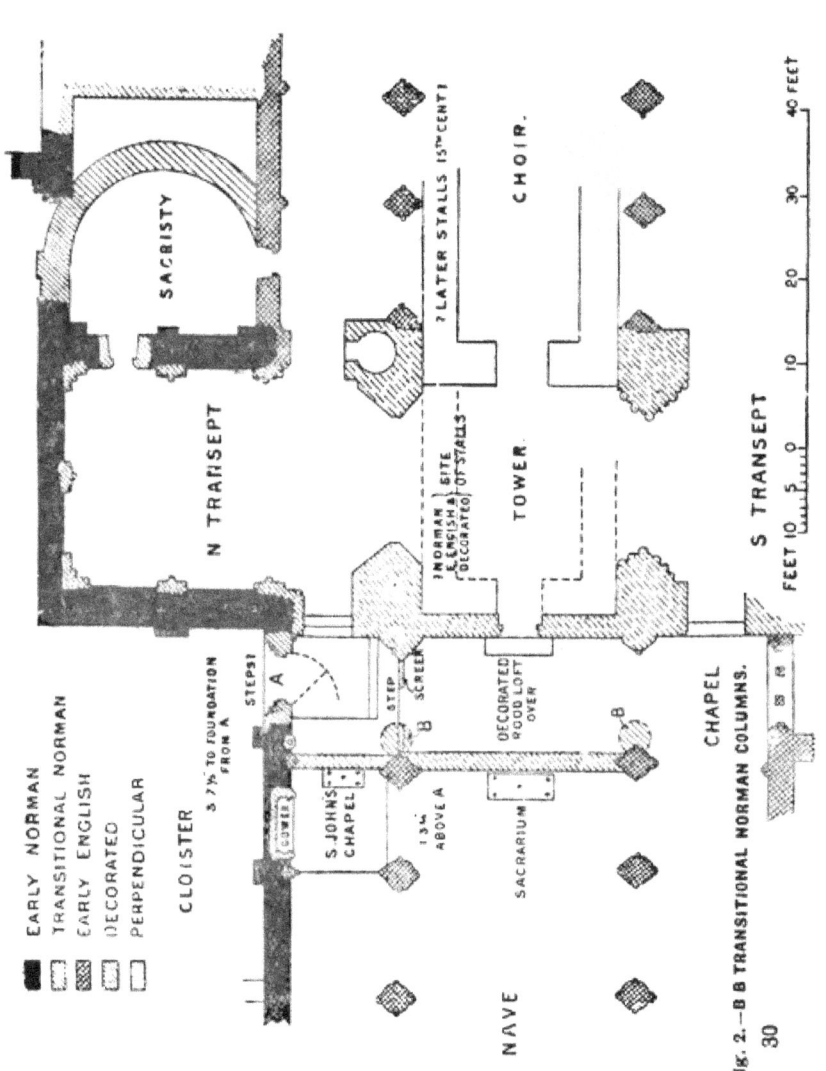

Fig. 2.—B B TRANSITIONAL NORMAN COLUMNS.

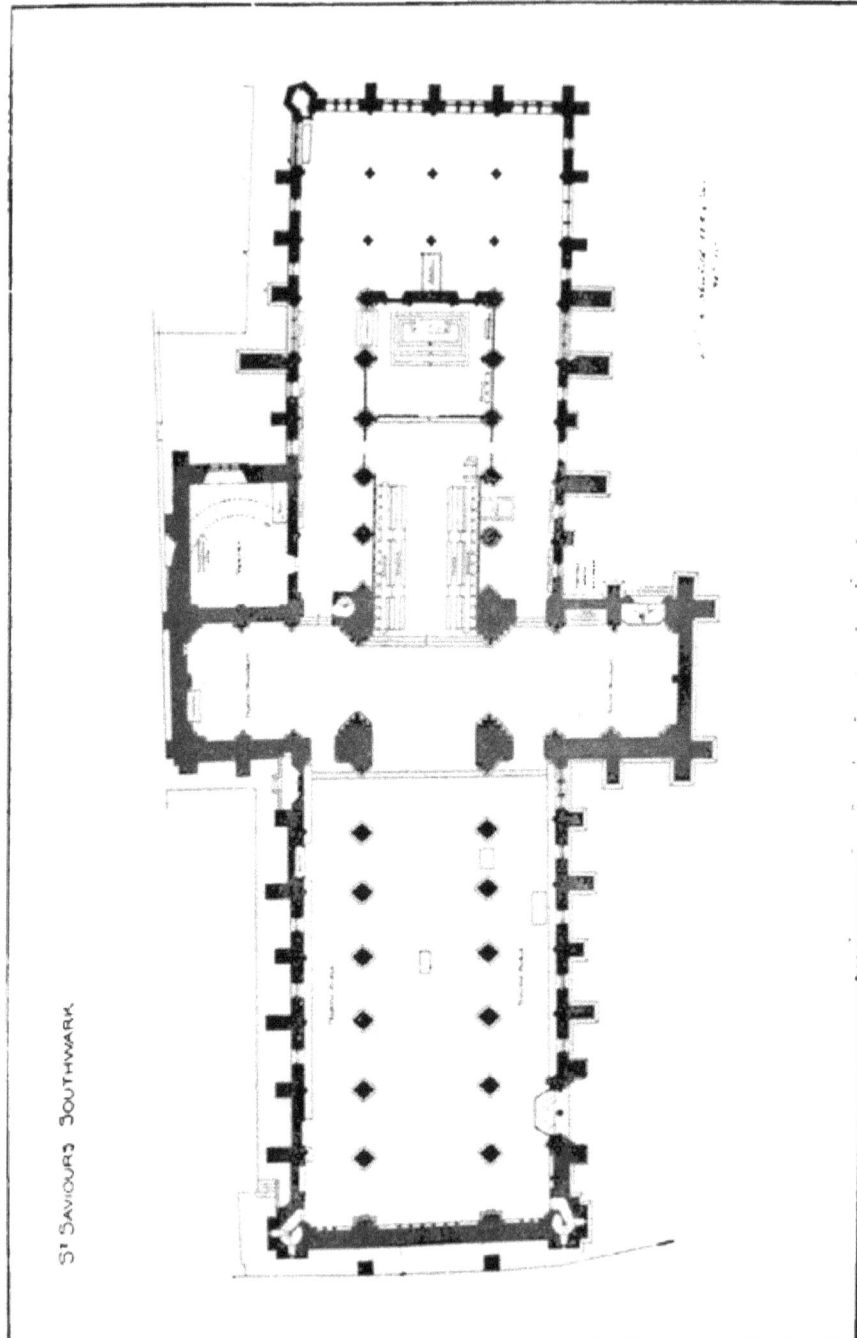

Genealogical Tree of Architecture.

Etruscan. Egyptian.

Early Roman. Greek.

—— Roman. ——

Romanesque. { Including Anglo-Saxon and Norman.

Gothic. { Including Early English, Decorated, and Perpendicular

Renaissance.

Etruscan.—Its salient feature was the semicircular arch, its most flourishing period B.C. 753; the Romans borrowed and absorbed it, thus forming the *Early Roman*.

Egyptian.—An imitation, originally in stone, of timber construction. Its salient features are the column and straight lintol.

Acknowledgments.

My acknowledgments are due for kind permission to use most of the foregoing Illustrations—

To the Proprietors of the *Graphic* for Nos. 4, 5, 6, 7.

To the *Daily Graphic* for Nos. 8, 25.

To *Black and White* for Nos. 18, 23.

To Messrs. Macmillan & Co.'s *English Illustrated Magazine* for Nos. 10, 11, 12, 20.

To the Council of the Royal Institute of British Architects for Nos. 29, 30.

To Messrs. Cassell & Co. for No. 24.

To Mr. Freeman Dovaston for Nos. 17, 28.

To the *Builder* for Nos. 13, 16.

To Messrs. Winkley & Son for No. 31.

W. T.

INDEX.

A	PAGE
Acknowledgments	75
Alleyne, Edward	57
Andrewes, Bishop	26
Anglican Martyrs	10, 23
Anne, Queen	39
Applebee, Dorothy	58
Architecture, Styles of	9, 22, 72
" Genealogical Tree of	75
Arms, Beaufort	11
" Priory	7
" Queen Anne	39
Augustinian (Austin) Canons	8
Aumbry	39, 40
Austin, William	43

B	
Baptistery	52
Baxter	9
Beaufort, Cardinal	8, 11
" Joan	10, 12, 54
Beaumont, dramatist	57
Becket, Archbishop	31
Bells	9
Benefield	13
Bingham	13
Bishops, consecrated	10
" three buried	9
Bonner, Bishop	23
Bosses, Carved Oak	21, 44
Bromfield, Lord Mayor	9
Bunyan	9

C	
Calvin and Servetus	25
Campbell, Lord, cited	31
Candelabra	58

	PAGE
Canons, Norman Doorway of	51
Canons, St. Saviour's	66
Chapel of our Ladye	21, 30
" of St. John the Apostle	37
" of St. John the Baptist	49
" Bishop's	30
" Little Ladye	30
" of St. Mary Magdalene	14, 70
" of St. Peter	40
Chaplains, List of	69
Chapter, The Collegiate	66
Charles I.	31
Chaucer	9
Chest, Muniment	44
Choir	60
"Church and State" Window	41
Cloisters	46
Cobham, Lady	54
Collar of SS	47
Consecrations	10
Creighton, Bishop, cited	31
Cross, Unique	40
" Consecration	46
" (see Gifts)	
Cruden	9
Crusader	33
Cure	34, 36

D	
Dimensions of St. Saviour's	9
Dollman, cited	22, 72
Doors, Norman	46, 51
Dorothea, St.	55
Dudley and Ward	33
Dugdale, cited	30
Duke of Connaught	16, 41, 58
Duke and Duchess of Teck	65

E

	PAGE
Elizabeth, Queen	10
Emerson, William	12
,, Ralph Waldo	12
Ethelbert, King	41

F

Fletcher, dramatist	10, 57
Font	52
Fox, Bishop	59
,, his Device	60
,, his Screen	59
Foxe, cited	25
Fuller, cited	26, 27, 28

G

Gardiner, Bishop	9, 10, 23
,, Dr. Rawson, cited	31
Gifford, Bishop	8
Gifts bestowed	63, 64
,, needed	65
Goldsmith, Oliver	9
Gower, the Poet	9, 10, 47
Gregory the Great	41
Gunpowder Plot	10
Gwilt, George	19

H

Harvard, John	10
,, University, U.S.A.	10, 15
Henry IV.	10, 53
Historical Summary	7
Humble, Alderman	32

I

Inscriptions, objectionable	30

J

James I. Scot.	10, 12, 54
"Jesse Tree"	13
Joan Beaufort	10, 12, 54
Joan of Kent	25
Johnson. Dr. Samuel	9

K

	PAGE
Kent, Earl of	10, 53
,, Joan of	25

L

Ladye Chapel	21
,, or Retro-Choir?	29
Langton, Archbishop	41
Laud, Archbishop	29, 31
Lease of Church	9
Lectern	59
Lockyer, Dr.	42

M

"Made in Germany"	24
Marriage, begun at Porch	10, 53
,, James I.'s (Scot.) (see James I.)	
,, Earl of Cumberland's	10
,, Earl of Kent's (see Kent)	
Martyrs, Chas. I., Becket, Laud	31
,, Marian (see Anglican)	
Massinger, dramatist	10, 55
Mayors, Lord, three buried	9
Merbeke	25
Morley, Prof. H., cited	50
Mozley, Prof., cited	31

N

Nave, The New	45
Newcomen, Elizabeth	16
Newland, Abraham	18
"Non-Such"	18
Norman Church, plans of	71, 73
,, Doorways	46, 51

O

Organ, The New	14, 70
Overie, Meaning of	7
Overs (Overy), John and Mary	38

P

Paulinus, St	52
Pelican, Device of	44, 60
Peter de Rupibus, Bishop	8

	PAGE
Pilgrim Fathers	25
Porch, South-West	54
Prince of Wales	9, 65
Princess of Wales	9
Princess Victoria	9
Princess Maud	9
Prince Arthur	16, 41, 58, 64
Princess Mary of Teck	65
Priors, List of	67
„ Norman Doorway of	46
„ and St. Thomas's Hosp.	31
„ Seal of	67
Pulpit (see Gifts)	

Q

Quair, The King's	54

R

Recess, Norman	51
Reopening Ceremony	65
Royalty at St. Saviour's	9, 16, 41, 58, 65

S

SS Collar	47
Sacheverell, Dr. Henry	10, 39
Sandall, Bishop	9
Screen, Altar	20, 59
„ Chancel (see Gifts)	
Servetus and Calvin	25
Shakespeare	55
„ A Parishioner	62
„ Edmond	10, 55, 62
Shorter, Sir John, Lord Mayor	
Spenser	55
Stalls (see Gifts)	
Stow, cited	7, 54
Stubbs, Bishop, cited	10
Swithun, St.	8, 52

T

	PAGE
Teck, Princess Mary and Duke of	65
Tessera	16
Times, The, cited	31
Tour of the Interior	11
Transept, North	38
„ South	11
"Tree of Jesse"	13
Trehearne	34, 37

W

Ward, Dudley and	33
Waterman, Lord Mayor	9
Wickham ii., Bishop	9, 62
Wykeham, Bishop William of	10, 41

Windows—

Commencing at the north-east side of the Ladye Chapel, proceeding down the north aisle of the Choir to the North Transept, passing round the Nave, into the South Transept, and halting in front of the High Altar.

Charles I., Becket, Laud	31
Prince Consort (Church and State)	41
Creator Mundi (West)	52
St. Swithun	52
St. Paulinus	52
Alleyne	57
Beaumont	57
Fletcher	57
Massinger	55
Shakespeare	55
Newcomen	16
"Jesse Tree"	13
Salvator Mundi (East)	64

www.ingramcontent.com/pod-product-compliance
Lightning Source LLC
Chambersburg PA
CBHW020338090426
42735CB00009B/1589